LAW for the
SMALL
BUSINESS

Contact Law

- Company formation
- Business disputes
- Employment
- Contracts & leases
- Intellectual property
- Mergers & acquisitions

> Contact Law has thousands of commercial solicitors across the UK covering all aspects of law

> We discuss your exact requirements and then quickly introduce you to the most qualified, competitively priced solicitor

> This ensures you get the legal advice you need, now and as your business grows.

Please see Chapter 2 – Getting Going

Contact us free on 0800 1777 167
www.contactlaw.co.uk/commercial

THE SUNDAY TIMES

LAW for the SMALL BUSINESS

An Essential Guide to all the Legal and Financial Requirements

12TH EDITION

PATRICIA CLAYTON

KOGAN
PAGE

London and Philadelphia

To Dennis, Richard, Jane and Charles
With love and thanks

First published in 1979 by Marchmont Publications Ltd under the title *Law for the Small Businessman*
Second edition 1981
Third edition 1982
Fourth edition 1984
Fifth edition 1987
Sixth edition 1988
Seventh edition 1991
Eighth edition 1995
Ninth edition 1998
Tenth edition 2001
Eleventh edition 2004
Twelfth edition 2007

Kogan Page Limited
120 Pentonville Road
London N1 9JN
United Kingdom

British Library Cataloguing in Publication Data

A CIP record for this book is available from the British Library.

ISBN-10   0 7494 4955 1
ISBN-13   978 0 7494 4955 1

Typeset by JS Typesetting Ltd, Porthcawl, Mid Glamorgan
Printed and bound in Great Britain by Thanet Press Ltd, Margate

Contents

Could Your Website be Employee of the Month?

As a business owner, you understand the importance of creating and maintaining a successful, high-performance team of employees. A company is only as good as the people who work for it, so it is only logical that you seek out the best employees with qualities that will make them, and in turn, you, successful. Good employees are your best asset – they help your business profit through their diligence, commitment, and expertise.

Most business owners realise the correlation between winning employees and a successful business, and spend a great deal of time, effort, and money to find and retain the best of the best to staff their company.

But, what about their website?

Many business owners don't recognise the similarities between high-performance employees and high-performance websites. If you compare the two, you'll see how similar they really are, and from there, you can take steps to help your business' website become your Employee of the Month.

Top 5 qualities of your best, high-performance employees:	Top 5 qualities of a high-performance website:
1. Strong and consistent work ethic	1. Consistently attracts traffic
2. Excellent interpersonal skills skills	2. High interactivity with site visitors visitors
3. Solid business fundamentals fundamentals	3. Reflects industry best practices and business knowledge
4. Ability to network effectively within the organisation	4. Link popularity and reciprocal link exchange
5. Ambition and desire to grow professionally	5. Ability to be updated with fresh content and tools.

1. Your best employees are those who perform consistently, and truly work for the company. If an employee does not work hard for you consistently, it's not likely that you would keep him or her on your team. The same principle should apply to your website. A great website works for your business, not against it. Your website, if optimised correctly for search engines and marketed effectively, will bring online visitors to you, and will help convert these visitors to customers. If it isn't working for you, why would you continue to employ it?

2. A great employee works well with your customers. So should your website work well with visitors to your site. Websites that are basic online brochures are simply not effective in this day of advancements in technology. An effective website should contain a wealth of resources for your customers, including downloadable resources such as white papers, answers to frequently asked questions, and opportunities to contact the company and offer feedback.

3. You expect your employees to understand what is required of them and to apply businesses fundamentals and best practices in their job. Your website should be no different. A website that is built to industry standards and utilises industry best practices for design and functionality will be effective and appreciated by your customers. Implementing best practices such as Web accessibility guidelines is simply a smart thing to do as the online world becomes more and more focused on the end-customer's needs.

4. Networking has long been an important part of business. Employees who network effectively are a great asset to you, since they will increase your visibility within the local market place. Effective websites apply the same principle through reciprocal link programs. Linking to another website that your customers would find beneficial, and having them link to you in return, increases your visibility in search engines like Google and Yahoo! Reciprocal link programs are beneficial to both businesses, and the added, pertinent links on the site are beneficial to the website user as well.

5. Your website, just like your employees, should change and evolve as its role in your business changes in order to ensure that their 'skills' do not become obsolete. Websites should be designed in a way that makes them easily updatable. If you do not update your website with current information and leading-edge technologies, your readers will become disenchanted with it and are less likely to return to it.

There is no doubt that in today's business world, having a strong online presence is important for any business. The e-business world is a level playing field, where small businesses can occupy the same amount of space and have the same impact as the big guys. Only when your website starts working for you as diligently and effectively as your best employees, will you see how much it can benefit your business. Why not make your website work harder for you?

WSI (We Simplify the Internet), one of the world's leading providers of Internet Solutions to small and medium sized businesses the world over, has over 1500 local Consultants in 87 countries who can help you make your website content a more effective tool for your business. WSI helps SMEs by creating Internet solutions that give them the **ABCs of Internet Marketing Success**™.

- The first step in the ABCs is **A**ffordable Website Design Solutions. Before your business can take full advantage of Internet marketing, you need to establish a presence online. When it comes to delivering Website Solutions, affordability and efficiency are two important concerns for us because they're important to our clients. We use cutting edge technology to design affordable business-class websites that need no technical staff to maintain, that generate revenue during all hours of the day and are easily found by consumers within our clients' target markets.

- The second step is **B**uild Targeted Website Traffic. Search engine marketing has become the most cost-effective way to reach your customers and offers unprecedented targeting capabilities. At WSI we use unique tools and business processes, combined with techniques like Web ads, Search Engine Optimisation, Guaranteed Inclusion advertising, among others, to ensure your business attracts the highest volume of targeted Web traffic possible.

- The third step is **C**onvert More Customers – with better website return on investment (ROI). Establishing a presence online and driving qualified traffic to your website are the first steps, and with those tasks complete, you can focus on the real work: turning those visitors into buyers.

If you would like to find out more about how WSI can help your business, please contact Stuart James, your local WSI Consultant at **StuartJames@wsiprowebconcepts.co.uk** or call **01753 574 822**. Stuart can help you learn how to make your website worthy of the "Employee of the Month" plaque.

Code 9 is a design agency collaboration of freelance designers and web developers with extensive knowledge of their fields. Services include corporate identity, business branding, web development and design for print.

Clients may find that with most design agencies they have to get past the receptionist, account manager and various other walls before they can speak directly to the designer who is working on their project. With Code 9 you cut out the middleman and deal direct with the designer to give you the best possible price.

Web Design and Development

In today's competitive business climate you cannot afford to neglect your business on the internet. The web is now almost the first point of contact when customers decide to check out your business. Your website is the doorway to thousands, if not millions of potential customers worldwide, therefore it has to be a major part of your business marketing strategy.

Code 9 design can create professional creative websites that sell your business and strengthen your brand, products or services, whether your business is a start-up, established business or individual concern. You can choose from a simple but beautiful brochure style website to a flash enhanced, content managed or ecommerce solution.

"We will treat each website individually as a bespoke project and build with the aim of transferring the clients' brand presence to the web", explains Jerry Holliday, head of web development. "We also optimise each site to give it the best possible chance of ranking well in the search engines and can guide the client to other methods and ways of driving visitors to their website".

Code 9 can also advise clients on their online marketing strategy as well as offline integration, pay-per-click advertising, legal disclaimers and competitive web hosting.

Business Branding

The corporate identity and branding of your business is quite possibly the most important aspect of your marketing strategy. First impressions do and will last!

Without a strong presence your business could drown under the competition and potential customers will never be able to connect and therefore never become real customers.

conversations

brew great concepts

talk directly to the designers

design for print | web design & development | corporate id & branding | design for packaging | illustration

Code 9 Design
tel | fax 0117 907 6220
www.code9.co.uk | info@code9.co.uk

Code 9 can help you develop a solid blueprint foundation on which to base your corporate identity message and give your business the maximum possible impact. They also understand that consistency in both printed and digital media is important in business communication to your customers.

Design for Print

You may need to promote your business through brochures, leaflets, directory adverts, newsletters and many other marketing methods. Code 9 can take your promotional materials from design and layout stage, right through to the finished printed product delivered straight to your doorstep. They have a long established relationship with trusted printers and can take care of all your business printing needs.

Whether you are a new or established business, Code 9 can offer you a very competitive deal including corporate identity (business letterhead, compliment slips and business cards) and a brochure website. Just visit **www.code9.co.uk/deal** for the latest competitive prices.

Preface

This is a 'how-to' – not 'do-it-yourself' – guide to your legal and financial responsibilities as an entrepreneur and employer: how to start your business, how to keep it going and how to avoid the legal pitfalls that beset your path. You are forewarned and forearmed but *not* equipped to be your own lawyer.

Chapter 1 outlines business structure. Later chapters deal with the impact of your choice of structure on various aspects of your business dealings. Some land, tax and insurance law and relevant areas of commercial law are covered as well as health and safety and employment legislation and litigation.

This is, however, a slimmed-down, easy-reference edition of the original *Law for the Small Business* and the law is set out in broad terms. If you run into problems you must dig deeper and consult legal and/or financial experts.

But the pile of legislation daily grows higher. In many areas ignorance is no defence and you cannot afford to risk yourself and your capital in the legislative jungle without some knowledge of the terrain.

It is now an offence under the Fraud Act 2006 to commit fraud by:

- making a dishonest false representation in words or conduct with the intent to make a gain or cause loss or risk to another;
- wrongfully failing to disclose information, eg where a professional advisor with a duty to safeguard clients' interests dishonestly profits from his or her position;

■ dishonestly abusing a position, eg where an employee clones an employer's software products in order to sell them to a competitor;

■ obtaining services dishonestly;

■ possessing articles, including computer programs, for use in fraud.

And the Act extends the offence of fraudulent trading to sole traders and partnerships.

Private companies, however, will have an easier time when the new Company Law Reform Bill comes into force in mid-2007. They will not be required to set authorised share capital, the statutory articles of association are shorter and the requirements for accounts and audits have been simplified. Restrictions on financial assistance to potential or actual shareholders to acquire or purchase private company's shares are to be removed and it will be easier to reduce the company's capital. Directors will be able to file a service address with Companies House instead of their private home address and their general duties are specified. Annual general meetings will no longer be mandatory and company decisions will only require a simple or 75 per cent majority vote on written resolutions.

A general note: our law is now part of the commercial and social law of the European Union, a common market for capital, labour and goods. EU law applies directly in the member states and cannot be altered or amended by reference to our earlier or later legislation. Common standards of quality and safety are being imposed on goods and services, procedures are becoming more open and increasing attempts are being made to reduce burdens on the smaller business.

The law stated is at November 2006 but the date label on the law is no indication that it is in force and some legislation is still in the process of being implemented. If in doubt, seek legal advice. Your local Citizens' Advice Bureau, Consumer Advice Centre, trade or employers' association or Chamber of Commerce may be able to advise you and various government departments publish useful and informative pamphlets.

Get started with start.biz

The name of a business is one of its most vital assets. It's how you answer the phone. It's how people remember you and your products or services. It's what they see in your advertising, your leaflets, your business cards and stationery. It's how your business gets recommended to others. It really is – **your business.**

Choosing the name that represents the service you are offering is one of the first and most important decisions in establishing your new enterprise. You can use almost any name you think conveys the right image for your business. However, there are limitations: statutory and legal obligations and other pitfalls that can be costly and time consuming if you don't research them thoroughly right from the start.

National Business Register can take you quickly, confidently and economically through this critical stage in setting up your enterprise - and then protect your chosen business name.

Get It Right At The Start

National Business Register operates the only UK search and protection service, which takes the time, effort, expense and risk out of choosing a name. Established in 1984, we offer a unique, national, private-sector business service that now protects tens of thousands of businesses.

National Business Register Plc is a name approved by the Secretary of State for Trade and Industry.

How Can I Register?

You can either contact us for an application form and post it to us in our pre paid envelope or complete free basic searches and apply online at **www.start.biz**

On receipt of your application form, **National Business Register Plc** will check that your name is legal (advising where changes are necessary) and search all business and company name databases (plus trade marks if requested). Once we are satisfied that your name can be used and that it does not conflict with any existing names, we will add it on the **National Business Register** database and prepare your certificate. This confirms the name is protected against passing off and, when displayed, it will meet all the display requirements of the Business Names Act 1985. In addition to these benefits, we also include a free helpline service that is open 24 hours a day, 365 days a year throughout the duration of your registration. This service provides you with free advice on legal matters, tax issues and also includes a confidential counselling service. You will also have access to the Businesslaw Service, which can provide you with a wide range of letters, articles and reference information, as well as interactive document builders, designed to help run your business.

Membership Costs and Further Services

Annual Membership of the National Business Register costs £60.00. Searches against trade marks are more complex than business names. A trade mark search can be undertaken for an additional fee of £80.00. If the business occupies more than one location, details must be displayed at each site. Additional certificates can be supplied for £8.00.

Limited Company Formation

National Business Register also offer limited company formation. The main benefits of this are that should a business fail, limited liability can protect the owner from personal loss, or even bankruptcy, which a sole trader could not avoid. Therefore the debts are the company's, not yours and your personal assets are protected.

We supply Private Limited Companies that are completely new and Tailor-made to your requirements, or Ready-made Companies with a name already registered with which you can trade immediately. We also form Public Limited Companies and Companies Limited by Guarantee.

When forming a company through **National Business Register,** we provide you with a professional company kit that includes the following: certificate of incorporation, 6 sets of memorandum and articles of association, fully completed statutory books, company register, share forms and minutes of the first meeting. All included in an attractive attaché case. Formations are completed electronically and only take 24 hours.

Domain Name Registration

We also provide a domain name registration service that includes services such as domain name registration, hosting and website design.

Registering a domain name will ensure that your business has a presence on the internet and will also ensure that your domain name cannot be stolen by a competitor.

Full information detailing all of the services we offer can be found on our website:
www.start.biz Alternatively, you may contact us on **0870 700 8787**
and one of our highly trained advisors will be on hand to help.

Starting out

Going into business can be simple enough but the financial implications are complicated. Independence is tempting, partnership has its pitfalls and behind the facade of many a private limited liability company is an entrepreneur as fully exposed to outrageous business misfortune as the sole trader.

The choice of business structure, however, is essential to the way you operate. It is the legal framework within which is determined your share of profits and losses and your responsibilities to associates, employees, creditors and anyone investing in your expertise.

Choices

Sole trading

The sole trader is the ultimate entrepreneur. You put your own money on your own expertise, taking out and putting into the business as much money and time as you choose and you are financially committed to the extent of everything you own. If you fail, creditors can demand payment in full, seizing and selling everything you own, including most personal possessions, or making you bankrupt.

Personal assets can be put beyond the reach of business creditors – for instance, assets can be put into relatives' names with the proviso that they invest in the business – but this reduces flexibility. They may not stand by you and transferring the family home into your spouse's or partner's name can be disastrous if you end up in the courts. Also, there may be liability for tax and/or stamp duty and some transactions can be set aside if you go bankrupt or defraud creditors. You should therefore seek expert advice before taking action.

Partnership

Partners share problems and profits but the price may be high. The partnership is not a separate legal 'person'. Partnership law is being reviewed, particularly the problems arising from lack of independent legal personality, the break up of the business on change of ownership and the partners' unlimited liability, but currently you, your partners and the business stand or fall together and an insolvent partner can put the partnership out of business. Partners are jointly and severally liable for all the partnership's commercial obligations, although you are responsible only for your partners' dishonest acts if you are involved in them. When you leave the partnership, you take financial responsibility with you unless you publicly announce the split by notifying business contacts and advertising it in the official *Gazette*.

Partnerships can be based on oral, informal agreements but the law puts a full agreement together if details are not specified. It is therefore best to have a formal, signed and witnessed, agreement. This sets the pattern of your current and future financial life and you should take legal advice before finalising it, so that you and your partners fully understand its implications.

Sleeping partners have the same liability as other partners even if their only involvement is investment in the business in return for a share of profits.

Limited partnership

Partners can put limits on financial commitments but at least one partner must have unlimited liability for business debts. The limited partner has limited rights and can only give general advice, and involvement in the business brings unlimited liability. Essentially the position is that of a lender to the business receiving interest at a rate varying with profits. But the limited partner is not a creditor and can only resign with the other partners' consent, unless other arrangements are agreed.

Limited partnerships must be registered with the Companies Registrar. Registration costs £2 and the Registrar must be notified of changes within 15 days. Details of the limitation and/or change must also be sent to the *Gazette*.

Limited liability partnerships (LLPs)

An LLP is organised like a partnership, but the members (partners) have limited liability. Their duties are specified and include those usually carried out by company directors or secretaries – for instance, signing and filing annual accounts and putting together the statement of business affairs in insolvency.

Disclosure requirements are similar to a company's, including the requirement to file annual returns and notify changes in membership, changes of members' names and addresses and a change in the Registered Office address.

Like companies, LLPs are legal entities separate from their members, so the LLP is liable to the full extent of its assets and members have limited liability. Third parties will usually contract with the LLP rather than with members, but individual members may, in some circumstances, be liable for negligence.

Incorporation is achieved by registration at Companies House and costs £20. Members provide the working capital and share the profits. Income is treated similarly to partnership. The LLP is taxed as a partnership and members pay Class 1 and Class 4 NICS.

Partnerships converting to LLPs receive relief from stamp duty on property transferred in the first year, subject to conditions. New and existing partnerships of two or more persons can incorporate as LLPs but not an existing company.

Franchising

A franchise agreement licenses the franchisor's goodwill through an agreement with the franchisee, who can be a sole trader, partnership or company. The franchisor gives ongoing support and advice, licensing a package of rights – for instance, copyrights, patents and know-how – and monitoring the franchisee, mainly by financial and quality controls. The franchisee pays a fee plus royalties and/or dividends. The franchisee owns the business but must conform with 'house-style' and the franchisor has ultimate control.

The franchise agreement must comply with both UK and EU law relating to unfair competition, and restraint of trade and the law is complicated. You are therefore advised to consult specialists in the field.

Limited companies

Trading as a private limited liability company enables you to enjoy the profits of the business while distancing yourself from its debts and obligations. The company can be formed with one shareholder/director but he or she cannot also be the company secretary.

Incorporation

Incorporating business activities brings the business to life as a separate legal person. Corporate structure facilitates outside investor participation and expansion. Debts are the company's debts and business goes on in spite of the resignation, death or bankruptcy of management and shareholders.

The fastest route to incorporation is to buy a ready-made 'off-the-shelf' company from a registration agent. Existing shareholders resign in favour of your shareholders and you appoint your own director and secretary. You can change the company name but first check to see that the 'objects' clause of the Memorandum – which covers the activities of the business – fits your business.

You can register a brand new company with Companies House but it involves delays, extra documentation and advertisement in the *Gazette*. The ready-made procedure is straightforward and faster but there are technicalities and you should seek professional advice before buying.

The Memorandum and Articles of Association

Your company is 'limited by shares' and the Memorandum states you are in business to make a profit and that the liability of the members (shareholders) of the company is limited to the nominal value of their shares. The Articles set out the shareholders' rights and obligations.

Directors, shareholders and limited liability

Whoever subscribes for and holds company shares must pay the company for them and responsibility for company debts is limited to the nominal (face or par) value of their shares. If they are fully paid up, the company cannot call on them again, even if the business is insolvent. It is the directors and management who are responsible to the company, shareholders and creditors but, unlike sole traders and partners, only in specified circumstances. If they do not go beyond the limits of the authority given by the company's Memorandum and Articles and act honestly and reasonably, creditors' claims can only be made against company assets.

Unlimited company shareholders are liable for all company debts, although creditors must go to court before they can obtain payment. Small limited companies can now file unaudited accounts with Companies House and do not have to file a directors' report, so the dispensation absolving unlimited companies from the requirement to file certain reports and accounts is less attractive.

EU law

Community law applies directly in the UK and cannot be altered or amended by reference to our own earlier or later legislation. Changes to our company law mainly apply to public companies but community law has had and continues to have a major impact on our commercial and consumer legislation.

Loans

Sole traders can reduce or increase business capital as they please. Partners can borrow and lend to the business as agreed among themselves. Some complicated legal provisions, however, stand between company directors and business capital for loans over £10,000 and sometimes they also need the shareholders' consent.

KEEPING YOUR NEW BUSINESS LEGAL

When you decide to set up a business you are often excited by the prospect, perhaps nervous about how things will turn out but rarely fascinated with the legal requirements. But failure to set your business up in a legally sound way could bring problems much further down the line.

There are six critical issues you need to consider. Here's a useful checklist of questions to ask yourself as you set up and run your business.

Business Structure

This is really one of the first decisions to make and one your accountant will certainly want to discuss with you. How do you want to operate: as a sole trader, in partnership or as a limited company? Your decision will be made after consideration of a number of factors but without proper consideration you could make the wrong choice and your ability to develop your business might be restricted.

You might ask yourself the following questions:

1. How much personal liability am I willing, or is it appropriate, to take for the business?
2. Will I be dealing with established or 'big' companies who will expect the apparent credibility of limited company status?
3. Might I be financially better off as a director of my own limited company rather than as a sole trader?
4. Do I need to raise finance from a variety of sources to get my business off the ground or allow it to grow?
5. Might I want to sell all or part of the business in the future?

Doing Business

In pretty much every business you can think of you buy things in (whether that's services, supplies, products or labour), make sales and (all being well) receive payment. Whilst simple in principle, all three of these areas are fraught with potential difficulty if you are not prepared.

You should consider:

1. The terms of any agreements you enter into for buying supplies and services, looking carefully for small print on what happens if deadlines are missed, or if the things supplied are not up to the required standard. What will happen, for example, if your web developer fails to deliver your website up to standard or by the date required and you've paid 50% of the cost up front?
2. How do you plan to do business – on-line, face to face or via mail order? Each has its own set of legal requirements and on-line trading particularly can be a minefield for the uninitiated.
3. Your own terms and conditions of business – what length of credit are you willing to give customers? What penalties do you need to have in place if they fail to pay your invoices? Do you need and are you able to limit your liability for

the products or services that you sell? When will you ask customers to sign or agree to your terms of business?

4. Where will your own business be in the 'production' chain? Will you be a supplier of other people's goods, an assembler of parts, a manufacturer or a business that provides services only? How will a problem further up or down the 'chain' affect you?

5. Are there any particular legal requirements or regulations peculiar to the industry in which you will set up your business?

Taking on Employees

As soon as you take on your first employee you open yourself up to a whole raft of employment legislation and potential penalties for getting things wrong. Even advertising for employees is fraught with difficulties. It's no longer acceptable for example to advertise for an office junior or a trainee who needs to be 'young and enthusiastic.'

Consider the following points:

1. What rules are needed to control employee's use of email and the internet? You won't be able to discipline an employee for misuse unless they are made aware of your policy.

2. Do you need a restrictive covenant in your contracts to protect you from a member of staff leaving, with customer details, to work for a competitor?

3. Are you fully versed in the statutory procedures for grievance and disciplinary matters? If not you should familiarise yourself with these rules or you could land yourself in deep water if you have a member of staff who doesn't perform and you do not handle the situation in accordance with those rules.

4. Have you written procedures and policies for health and safety, fire evacuation and equal opportunities?

Sales and Marketing

You'd perhaps think that with carefully worded terms and conditions in place you are pretty much covered from this point of view. Not at all. Most businesses today have some form of web presence. Whether your new business will have a web presence simply for advertising or for e-commerce, customer data will be collected. Accumulation of customer information can provide a very valuable business asset when identifying market trends but the collection and management of such information is hedged around with significant rules and restrictions by the Data Protection Act.

The questions to consider here include:

1. Is your website legally compliant? For example if you collect details through an enquiry form or subscription offer are you handling this data legally?

2. Is your website clear and accessible to all potential users? Does it clearly state the terms upon which visitors to the site may use it? Is there a 'privacy policy' advising users as to what may happen to their data?

3. Do you store customer details? If so, you will probably need to be registered

with the Information Protection Commissioner and you will have to understand your responsibilities in relation to this data.

4. If you sell goods or services through the site, are the terms of those sales accessible to a buyer and properly incorporated into your agreement to do business with that buyer? Do these terms comply with the rules applicable to on-line sales?

All of these considerations come in to play before you should even take your first order.

Protecting Your Ideas

No doubt you have an idea for the name of your business and will want to develop an identity through a logo and business stationery. If you have developed a unique product or service this will also be valuable intellectual property which needs to be protected.

Ask yourself:

1. Have you checked that your company name isn't registered to another business?
2. Are you infringing anyone else's copyright, trade marks or design rights?
3. Have you ensured that everyone with whom you've shared your new product details has been asked to keep it confidential? A confidentiality agreement may be appropriate before you reveal details to another party.
4. Will you own the design or copyright in all the creative work that you commission (website and logo design for example) or will the designer own it because you failed to agree otherwise?
5. Do you know what intellectual property you have and how it may be protected?

Keep up to Date

Once you are in business you need to keep abreast of changes in the law. Changes are due in 2007 for example as a result of the Companies Act 2006, which are likely to impact on the directors of limited companies.

With everything else going on in your business it can be difficult to keep up to date, but failure to do so could create real problems. You should ask your lawyer to alert you to relevant changes so that there are no nasty surprises.

The following websites will help:
www.dti.gov.uk
www.bcentral.co.uk
www.business-lawfirm.co.uk

Article written by: Andrew Woolley, small business owner and lawyer.
Andrew established the UK's first virtual law firm, Woolley & Co, solicitors in 1996.

When the business borrows money, sole traders' and partners' contingent liability – that is, their ultimate responsibility for business debts – is enlarged accordingly. Loans to the company do not affect the directors' and shareholders' contingent liability and additional shareholders and debenture-holders buy a share of existing and future profits but, like any other lender, their only claim is against company assets.

Retaining control

Partnership or company, the majority rules the business. Without the protection of a shareholders' agreement, majority shareholders can often ride roughshod over minority shareholders' and dissenting directors' objections. Unless otherwise agreed, however, the resignation of dissenting partners dissolves the partnership and in some circumstances a partner can only be bought out or forced out in accordance with the terms, if any, set out in the partnership agreement.

Formalities

Sole traders and partnerships trading in their own names can simply open their doors for business. Paperwork and administration are their own – and the VAT and tax inspectors' – business and the partnership agreement is mainly for the protection and information of the partners.

Partnerships and companies must present accounts in a prescribed form, have an annual audit and keep certain registers. Companies and LLPs must file accounts and annual returns, listing changes made during the year, with the Companies Registrar. Unlimited companies do not have to file reports and accounts but they must send in the annual return. Documents filed with the Registrar are available for public inspection. There is therefore some inevitable publicity for even the smallest company.

Dealing with Companies House

You can now incorporate your limited liability partnership or company by filing the necessary documents electronically through incorporation agents. After incorporation you can register your business name and keep Companies House informed electronically yourself and download company and other searches. Details of the system can be found on the Companies House website (www.companieshouse.org.uk).

Close companies

There is a tax disadvantage for family and director-controlled companies controlled by up to five 'participants' and their 'associates'. Associates include family and nominee shareholders. Participants – that is, anyone with a claim to the company's income or capital – pay additional income tax on some fringe benefits and both participants and associates are liable for income tax on loans.

If loans were made to participators during an accounting period you must notify Her Majesty's Revenue & Customs (HMRC – also referred to as the Revenue) that the company is a close company and there could be liability to tax.

Tax comparisons

Sole traders, partners, directors and partnerships pay income tax; companies pay corporation tax. Trading on your own account takes assessment to tax from Schedule E to Schedule D, from the category of an employee to the self-employed. Schedule E taxpayers are taxed at source under PAYE and must fight for tax concessions after tax has been deducted. The Schedule D taxpayer has more control over income, outgoings and tax and, if well advised, can usually retain more earnings.

Sole traders and partners pay the lower self-employed rate of National Insurance contribution in Class 2 and Class 4. Company directors pay Class 1 contributions as employees and the company contributes as employer. The amount is a percentage of income and varies depending on whether or not the employment is contracted-out.

Are you starting up or already running a small business and need free legal advice?

The Law Society

Legal pitfalls have been the downfall of many promising businesses. The Law Society offer you the opportunity to receive a FREE HALF-HOUR initial consultation with one of our many regional *Lawyers For Your Business* members.

Call *Lawyers For Your Business* for advice on a range of legal issues, including:

- Finance
- Taxes
- Insurance
- Cash flow
- Company structure
- Franchising
- Employment
- Business premises
- Contracts
- Health & safety

For a list of solicitors in your area
call **020 7405 9075**

email lfyb@lawsociety.org.uk
www.lfyb.lawsociety.org.uk

LAWYERS FOR YOUR BUSINESS

Many business start-ups wouldn't dream of starting to trade without an accountant, but think of engaging a solicitor only when there is a crisis, even though early legal advice can help organisations avoid problems and save money.

A solicitor can help you identify potential problems and put measures in place to prevent them – to protect your business from risk, and save you money.

The Law Society's *Lawyers For Your Business* scheme is designed to provide start-up and small to medium-sized businesses with access to specialist business-related legal advice and offers a free initial half hour consultation with a solicitor. The scheme represents 1,000 member firms across England and Wales.

Contact the Law Society to obtain a list of solicitors in their area to set up an appointment. E-mail **lfyb@lawsociety.org.uk** or call **020 7405 9075**.

Some key pointers to assist those setting up in business make the most effective use of a solicitor:

Use an expert
A practice which handles conveyancing might not be best suited to handling commercial issues. Members of *Lawyers For Your Business* are experienced in business-related legal work, including employment matters, company structure, contracts, leases and copyright issues, i.e., how to protect ideas. If the need is very specialised, it is advisable to do some research on **www.solicitors-online.com**, which lists contact details and areas of specialism of all solicitors' practices across England and Wales.

Don't cut corners
Standard or 'off the shelf' documents can be a false economy. They rarely meet the needs of the business and can be found to be inadequate when disputes arise. It is far better to have tailor-made legal documentation drawn up by an expert who understands the business.

Clarify costs at the outset
The initial *Lawyers For Your Business* consultation is free, however, it is important that you clarify at the outset an estimate of costs before you decide to proceed. You should ask for a forecast of how costs will change in various eventualities, for example, if a matter goes to court.

Don't be intimidated
Don't be afraid to say when you don't understand. All specialists use jargon at some point without realising it, so don't worry about seeking clarification of legalese.

The scheme produces a *Plain English A-Z Guide to Business and Financial Terms* which defines some of the more regularly used terms setting up in business.

Prevention

Be proactive when seeking legal advice – don't wait for legal problems; prevent them happening in the first place. For example, many employment disputes arise out of poorly drafted service contracts or dismissal procedures that do not conform to statutory requirements.

Free self-help guides

The scheme has produced a set of seven step-by-step guides:

- ❖ **Starting Up in Business** – Discusses areas such as licences, insurance financing your business and franchising.
- ❖ **Employing Staff** – Are you aware of the restrictions imposed by employee privacy laws and the Human Rights Act? Is your tax treatment of temporary staff watertight? Do you have clear written procedures in the event of having to dismiss staff?
- ❖ **Contracts with Customers and Suppliers** – Do you know that tighter laws from the EU on unfair contract terms apply if you sell to the public? Do you confirm in writing all telephone agreements or changes over the phone to written terms? Are you relying on a copy of somebody else's terms, which may be defective inappropriate or illegal? Does your contract exclude liabilities for say, your own negligence?
- ❖ **Taking on Leased Business Property** – Have you checked that you have planning permission to use the premises for your type of business? Have you checked the rent review clause carefully? Is it fair enough? Do you know what is accepted practice for the terms of the lease, taking into account type and market conditions?
- ❖ **Raising Money for Your Business** – If you are a sole trader or partnership, are you prepared for all your personal assets to be put at risk if a loan cannot be repaid? Can you take advantage of the small business loan guarantee scheme? Do you know the true worth of the business?
- ❖ **Structuring Your Business** – Do you know what will be the effect on the business if a shareholder or director/partner dies unexpectedly? Do you need to protect your personal assets from unpredictable liabilities eg, being sued by a client? Do you wantto give or sell staff a key stake in the business?
- ❖ **Health & Safety at Work** – Are you aware of your duty of care to visitors? Have you taken into account the consequences of successful civil suits against employers for 'new' occupational injuries such as Repetitive Strain Injury and Work Related Stress? Are you logging all staff injuries and reporting serious ones?

Lawyers For Your Business is administered by the Law Society of England and Wales and is backed by Business in the Community, the Federation of Small Business and the Forum of Private Business.

www.lfyb.lawsociety.org.uk   **www.lawsociety.org.uk**

Sole traders and partners are personally liable for tax on business profits. The company is responsible for its own tax bill and, unless it is a close company, directors and shareholders pay tax only on their own earnings.

Closing down

Sole traders and partners can simply close the doors on the business but unless they sell out completely – and selling the business can be a complicated matter – the ghost of business failure can follow them into the bankruptcy court.

It is easier to buy and sell shares in your company. If the company or LLP is insolvent, business assets must be liquidated to meet creditors' claims, although creditors have no claim on personal assets unless fraud is proved or there are personal guarantees.

Quick comparisons

Although there are legal restrictions on companies and LLPs, the difference between trading as a sole trader, a partnership or a company is often only one of machinery.

Some concessions have already been made but the life of an LLP and company is expensive. When the new Company Law Reform Act comes into force in, it is hoped, mid 2007 private companies will have an easier and less expensive time. But LLPs and companies will still have to comply with the LLP and Companies Acts and the documents filed with Companies House, which currently include annual accounts and details of members' and officers' salaries, are of course open to public inspection.

But LLPs are not subject to the *ultra vires* rule, which binds companies to the stated 'objects' in the Memorandum of Association (see page 27), so that they are free to pursue any business venture with the agreement of the majority of the partners. They have no share capital and are therefore not subject to company law rules governing the maintenance of capital.

Sole traders and partners, including the partners in an LLP, therefore lead less complicated legal lives and can generally choose their own route to success or failure.

The advantages of limited liability and flexibility given to the partners in an LLP are, however, counterbalanced by the lack of privacy, the need for an LLP agreement and legal uncertainty – the structure is new to our law and all eventualities have not yet been covered. Shareholders in private limited companies are in a similar position, but they are not bound by an LLP agreement and the company operates within a well-developed and sophisticated legal structure.

However, unless you have attached restricted voting rights to shares, a bare majority of your company's shareholders can dictate policy, appoint and set directors' salaries, declare dividends and, subject to rather unclear limitations, ratify the acts of directors. Tax is no longer charged at a lower rate on profits retained in the company than the rate charged on the business income of sole traders and partners, regardless of what they drew in cash, and even limited liability is illusory if you are called upon personally to guarantee business debts.

Statutory references

Companies Act 1985
European Communities Act 1972
Limited Liability Partnership Act 2000
Limited Partnership Act 1907
Partnership Act 1890
Single Market Act 1987

and see statutory references to Chapter 6.

CODDAN CPM LIMITED

From England to the US, Mauritius to Hong Kong, Belize to Panama, we are one of the leading companies in the industry of International Business Incorporation.

We provide

- a new-business incorporation service which offers same day company formation,
- a fast, hassle free application process,
- competitive prices.

➤ We offer professional assistance and advice in the areas of business establishment, development, financial planning, increasing finance, corporate recovery, payroll, and personnel services.

➤ Working worldwide, we specialise in the incorporation of Private Companies, Public Companies, and Partnerships in England, Wales, Scotland, Northern Ireland, and the Republic of Ireland; Sociedades Limitadas (SL) and Sociedades Anónimas (SA) in Spain; Corporations (Inc.) and Limited Liability Companies (LLC) in the United States. We also incorporate international business entities in offshore locations, and hold a portfolio of ready-made companies which are ready to trade.

In addition to the incorporation of your company, Coddan provides other services such as:

Business structure and pacification • Legal advice • Nominee Director, Nominee Secretary, Nominee Share holder • Registered Address • Virtual office (telephone numbers, fax numbers, office space etc) • Notarizations • Apostilles • Name Registrations • Trademarks • Business Bank Accounts • VAT Registration • Accounting • Web services (design, host)

For more information go to:
www.ukincorp.co.uk or email **info@ukincorp.co.uk**
freephone **(0) 800.081.1510**

Worldwide company incorporation

Coddan CPM LTD is a leading independent firm with offices in London, Malaga, Delaware, New York City, Cologne, Cyprus and Honk Kong.

We provide new business incorporation service, offering same day company creation with hassle/free applications. We offer professional assistance and advice in the areas of business establishment, development, financial planning, increasing finance, corporate recovery, payroll, and personnel services.

Our experienced team is dedicated, proactive and focussed on finding rapid solutions. We specialise on incorporating Private Companies, Public Companies and Partnerships (in England, Wales, Scotland, Northern Ireland and The Republic of Ireland); Sociedades Limitadas (SL) and Sociedades Anónimas (SA) in Spain; American Corporations (Inc.) and Limited Liability Companies (LLC) in The United States. Additionally we incorporate International Businesses in Offshore countries, as well as provide Ready Made companies ready to trade.

Coddan assists new and existing business ventures in United Kingdom and abroad, incorporates companies internationally, plans business structures, assists on the opening of Business Bank Accounts, drafts documentation and legal statements, provides advice on acquisitions and disposals of UK property and other services.

Some of the countries where Coddan incorporates companies are England and Wales, Spain, Portugal, Germany, Unites States, Cyprus, Seychelles, the British Virgin Islands, Mauritius, Guernsey, Belize, Nevis, Panama, Hong Kong, and many others.

Other services we provide include: Business structure and pacification, Legal advice, Nominee Director, Nominee Secretary, Nominee Share holderRegistered Address, Virtual office (telephone numbers, fax numbers, office space), Notarizations, Apostilles, Name registrations, Trademark registrations, Business Bank Accounts, VAT Registration, Accounting, Web services (design, host).

2

Getting going

The sole trader for the most part goes his or her own way. If you take on partners, disagreement between the partners can force a winding up of the business and you need the protection of ground rules set out in a partnership agreement. As director of a limited company or partner in an LLP you may be even more restricted because you must comply with the LLP and Companies Acts.

Business names

Sole traders and *partners* can trade in their own names or under an additional name indicating they have taken over an existing business. Any other name must be registered with the Registrar of Companies. Almost any name is acceptable unless prohibited or misleading and Notes for Guidance are obtainable from Companies House.

Limited partnerships and *limited liability partnerships* must file the partnership name with the Registrar of Companies. The name must not 'offend' the Secretary of State or be a name the use of which would constitute a criminal offence. Again, suitable names are set out in the Notes for Guidance available from Companies House.

Unless you trade in your own name, the business name and your name must be on all business documents with an address at which service of documents concerning the business is accepted. The business name must also be displayed prominently at business premises. Anyone who does

Why is Finding the Right Solicitor So Important?

If you think you can save money by not seeking any legal advice as a young business then think again. Small businesses that decide they can manage without legal advice often find this to be a false economy when a legacy of poorly-drafted contracts and badly-kept company documentation comes back to haunt them in later years.

The importance of hiring a solicitor and hiring the *right* solicitor should not be underestimated. Solicitors not only produce the necessary documents to set you on your way, e.g. company formation documents, leases, terms and conditions, trademarks and employment contracts, but it's likely that they will advise you on other commercial issues as your business develops, for instance regarding acquisitions, debt collection and intellectual property. As such, a company should plan to work with the solicitor for several years and take the time to find a solicitor who will be suitable for their needs as the business grows. Therefore you should thoroughly research the credentials of the solicitor you hire to make sure they really do have knowledge of your industry and experience delivering the type of advice you require. Not all solicitors are experienced in commercial law although many generalist High Street solicitors will happily 'turn their hand' to advising companies in between working on wills or conveyancing clients. Hence, the difference between a good and bad solicitor is a lot greater than you would imagine and the need to find a real commercial law expert is essential otherwise the cost to your business can be significant in legal fees, litigation risk and wasted management time if you make a poor choice.

The Difficulty in Finding and Choosing the Right Commercial Solicitor

There are two key reasons why it is difficult to find the right solicitor for your business: firstly, the uniqueness of your company and the legal services it requires; and secondly, the difficulty in evaluating the expertise, customer service levels and price of a solicitor.

1. Every business is unique, not just in the products and services it provides, but also in the characters of the individuals who collectively represent it. A manufacturer of household products will clearly need different legal expertise from an e-commerce retailer. Equally though, two identical firms might still want

different solicitors for the same job due to more 'human' factors, one preferring an aggressive lawyer and one wanting a more studied approach. Finding the ideal solicitor is made harder by the fact that there are thousands of firms, many of whom are extremely small with a limited range of legal expertise.

2. As with all professions it's difficult to evaluate alternative suppliers.

For example, once you have found two commercial contract solicitors how do you know which one would be best? How do you know that they have the right expertise for you, that they will respond swiftly and efficiently to your requests and that they will be honest in calculating the fees they charge you?

So, What are the Options for Choosing a Solicitor?

Traditionally, many businesses have chosen based on a recommendation from a friend or business contact who has used a solicitor before. While this does provide some reassurance that the solicitors firm will be reliable and trustworthy, it does not mean it will have the specific expertise you will need. For example, a solicitors firm that helped your friend's business acquire another company won't necessarily be the best choice to help you fight a copyright dispute.

Equally, many businesses will contact a selection of local solicitors and try to assess which have the right expertise for their particular requirement. While this might get you closer to finding the solicitor with the right expertise, it will be difficult to know whether the firm will do the work quickly and efficiently, without overcharging you. It will also be very time consuming.

Given these difficulties, in 2004 the Government opened up the legal market to third party 'referral' companies such as Contact Law that would quickly introduce private individuals and businesses to the right solicitor(s) for their specific needs. This would also have the benefit of stimulating competition, as the best value solicitors would be much easier to find.

A Faster, More Effective Way of Choosing a Solicitor

Contact Law has developed its business model as a **'legal brokerage'**, assembling a UK nationwide network of over 200 approved law firms that it is quickly able to access to meet the needs of its clients.

When a business first gets in touch with Contact Law we assign a dedicated case handler to take responsibility for that business and ensure that it gets the legal advice required in the necessary timeframe.

Our case handlers will explore our client's requirements for legal advice around four key criteria:

- **Expertise** – what specialist knowledge is the business looking for, e.g. property, contracts, copyright, etc?

- **Price** – is there a realistic budget and what pricing structure is required, i.e. hourly billing, fixed fee or no-win-no-fee? Is the lowest possible price wanted, or more of a balance between price and experience?

- **Location** – is a local solicitor required, or is the business happy to liaise with the solicitor via email, phone and fax?

- **Timescale** – how quickly does the work need to be done?

Once this is understood, the case handler can offer tailored **independent** advice to the business on its legal options and agree a way forward. Having consulted our database of 200+ law firms we will then quickly introduce them to a solicitor (or solicitors) able to meet the requirements. Once the business and solicitor have spoken, we will follow-up to check the client's feedback and introduce them to further solicitors if required. In most instances, this whole process is completed very quickly indeed, typically within 24 hours.

Through using Contact Law, not only are businesses assured that the potential solicitors have the right expertise, but they also know that they have been evaluated as cost-effective providers with high levels of customer service. Furthermore, like other brokers (such as mortgage brokers) Contact Law is paid for providing this service from the lawfirms' marketing budgets, such that there is no charge to the client. A win-win all round!

If you are looking for a solicitor, or have an existing or potential solicitor already who you wish to 'market-test', then we invite you to call Contact Law free on **0800 1777 167** or visit our website at **www.contactlaw.co.uk/commercial**. After all, you have nothing to lose and very much to gain by doing so....

business with you but does not visit the premises must be notified in writing of the business name and address.

The partners' names must be on letterheads. If there are more than 20 partners their names can be omitted, provided the address of the principal place is included and a list of partners' names is available there for inspection during office hours on payment of a reasonable fee.

Companies can use business names showing a continuing connection with the previous proprietor's business.

Companies and LLPs

A brand-new company's name costs £20 on application for incorporation. Changing the name costs £10.

The last word of a company name must be 'limited', or 'cyfyngedig' if the registered office is in Wales. The name must not be 'offensive' to the Secretary of State or one which, if used, would constitute a criminal offence or be the same or similar to that of an existing company.

The Registrar's Index of Company Names should be checked but it does not show pending applications. You may therefore have to make a change within 12 months of registration if the name is the same or 'too like' an existing company name. If the Secretary of State feels misleading information was given or undertakings and assurances given on registration are not met, he has five years during which he can direct that a change be made.

The Registrar reserves the name pending the passing of a special resolution of 75 per cent of the shareholders, a copy of which must be sent to the Registrar with the registration fee. The name cannot be used until you receive the Registrar's certificate and permission may be withdrawn before issue.

Directors are personally liable on contracts made before issue of the certificate and breach of the regulations applying to business and corporate names is a criminal offence.

The company or LLP's name, registered number, registered office address and the names of the directors or designated partners must be on all business documents, including formal notices, cheques, letters of credit, bills of exchange, promissory notes, endorsements, invoices, receipts and orders for money or goods signed by, or on behalf of, the company or LLP.

The LLP's letterhead must also state that it is a limited liability partnership. If there is more than one business address, you should specify which is the registered office.

The company or LLP's name must be prominently displayed at your main business premises, and LLPs must also display the name prominently and legibly outside their offices and places of business, including, if a place of business, a partner's home.

Domain names

You should also register a domain name on the internet (see page 196).

Trademarks

Trademarks must be separately registered with the Trade Marks Registry (see Chapter 11).

The partnership agreement

You should have a formal agreement executed in a deed (that is, signed and witnessed) to include:

■ **The partnership name and address and the nature of the business.** Business is usually done in the partnership name but implicitly entered into by all the partners, so they are directly liable for business activities. Partnership assets should be put in the partnership's name, or in the name of a maximum of four partners as trustees for the business, to differentiate business assets from personal assets.

■ **The date you start and end the partnership.** Fixed period partnerships continue unchanged after the stated date but a single business project partnership ends when the project is completed. If no fixed period or specific business venture is agreed, the partnership ends when a partner gives notice. It is best therefore to state that the partnership can only be terminated by mutual agreement.

■ **The amount of capital contributions.** No interest is payable on initial contributions, investments and advances unless stated in the agreement. You should specify whether interest is to be paid on initial contributions before profits are calculated.

■ **The bank account.** A statement of who can sign cheques and a provision that payments received for the business are paid into the partnership account.

■ **How profits are to be calculated and divided.** In the absence of this clause the partners are entitled to equal shares of cash received, less cash paid, without consideration of book and bad debts, whatever they initially put into the business. It is also advisable to include:
  – the spheres of activity of each partner;
  – whether part-time partners are to draw salaries instead of sharing profits;
  – a provision that drawings can be made against future profits;
  – what items, such as cars, not exclusively used for business, can be charged to expenses.

You may also want to specify a top limit on expenses and a figure above which no partner can enter into transactions without the other partners' consent.

■ **Accounts.** A provision requiring regular accounts and an annual balance sheet showing what is due to the partners in respect of capital, share of profits and salary.

■ **A clause** referring partnership disputes to arbitration.

■ **A clause** indemnifying a partner for claims arising from partnership activities.

■ **A clause** permitting arrangements to be made with creditors through the courts if there are cash flow problems (see page 227).

■ **Dissolution.** Failing agreement to the contrary, the partnership is automatically dissolved on a partner's retirement, death or bankruptcy. You should therefore specify how retiring and deceased partners' shares are to be valued and paid off. Alternatively, you can agree to pay an annuity out of profits.

An LLP's agreement should in addition set out:

- the names of the designated partners;
- which partners are to manage the business;
- the decision-making process;
- the capital contributions while the business is a going concern and (if any) on liquidation;
- dispute resolution;
- details of termination of the LLP;

and provision should be made for amending the agreement.

The agreement is binding and can only be altered with the consent of all the partners. *But* it is a private document recording agreement between the partners. If you are a partner with your name on the letterhead, you are responsible for the firm's actions, debts and liabilities unless outsiders are told you are not.

Points 2 and 9 above are important because, for some partnerships a change of partners is a discontinuance of the old partnership and a commencement of a new one for tax purposes. Discontinuance technically dissolves the partnership and the business is taxed as if you had stopped trading and begun again. Each partner is assessed on, and is solely responsible for, the tax on his or her share of partnership profits.

Incorporation: LLPs and companies

The incorporation documents obtainable from Companies House require:

- details of the LLP or company's name;
- the address of the registered office in England, Wales or Scotland;
- the LLP members' or company shareholders' and officers' full names, residential addresses, dates of birth and occupations.

LLPs must have at least two designated members with responsibilities similar to directors. A sole remaining member automatically acquires unlimited liability for partnership debts. If there are more than two members you must state whether two or all of them are to be designated members.

You can, however, be sole director of a company without taking on unlimited liability but you cannot then also serve as Company Secretary.

Partners and directors can apply to the Company Law and Investigations Directorate, 1 Victoria Street, London SW1H 0ET (Tel: 020 7215 0225) for a Confidentiality Order to permit them not to reveal their usual residential address and giving an alternative address for service of documents if they can show that disclosure would expose them to actual or serious risk of violence or intimidation. Some authorities, including the police, have access to the actual residential address. Details are also available on the Department of Trade and Industry's website dti.gov.uk. Special permission will not be required when the Company Law Reform Act comes into force.

The company's constitution

The *Memorandum of Association* sets out the company's basic constitution and its powers and duties as a legal person. Standard forms are available from The Stationery Office and Companies House, which can be tailored for your purposes before you apply for registration.

The Memorandum must state:

- the company's name which, if you are trading for profit, must include the word 'limited', or, if you are trading in Wales, the Welsh equivalent;
- that the registered office is in England, Wales or Scotland to establish domicile for tax purposes (names of some major cities are also acceptable);
- the objects for which the company is formed, that is a description of the company's objectives and powers and the field in which it does business. Transactions outside or not incidental or ancillary to the company's powers may be void as against the company under the *ultra vires* rules, although valid and enforceable against management;

- that the liability of shareholders is limited by (their) shares;
- the amount of initial nominal (or authorised) capital and how it is divided into shares (which fixes the fee payable on incorporation). *But* there is no requirement for authorised capital under the Company Law Reform Bill. The percentage which is subscribed in cash or asset value is the *issued capital*. Any unpaid balance is *uncalled capital* and shareholders' liability is limited to this amount if the company goes into liquidation;
- the names of subscribers (signatories) to the Memorandum and that they agree to take out at least one share each.

The Memorandum must be signed by at least two promoters or the promoter of a single member company – the 'subscribers' to the Memorandum – who must give their full names, address and occupation. If appropriate, they should apply for Confidentiality Orders but these will no longer be required when the Company Law Reform Bill comes into force.

The *Articles of Association* deal with internal organisation, the company's relationship with shareholders and their relationship with each other, the issue of share capital, the appointment and powers of directors and proceedings at meetings. Again, a standard form of Articles is available from The Stationery Office and Companies House. Shorter and simpler Articles of Association are to be introduced under the Company Law Reform Bill.

First business contracts

Organising the business prior to transferring it to a partnership or limited company transforms you into a promoter. The partnership and company must therefore consent to any profit you make from the sale of assets to them and full details of the transaction must be disclosed.

Selling to the partnership

When you sell to the partnership, the law assumes you act in good faith. You must therefore give your partners full details of any transactions you enter into that affect the partnership, both before and after its formation. The partners can make any arrangement concerning assets which remain the property of individual partners, but once it is agreed that an asset is to belong to the partnership, any increase or reduction in value belongs to the partnership.

Selling to the company

Promoters are personally liable in any transaction made on behalf of the company before incorporation unless there is specific agreement to the contrary. Promoters should therefore contract on the basis that they are no longer liable once the contract is put before the company's board of directors or the general meeting of shareholders, whether or not the company adopts the transaction. Once adopted, the preliminary contract is replaced by a draft agreement which is executed by the company on incorporation.

Alternatively, you can now enter into a contract for the benefit of your not-yet-incorporated company, provided that the company is specifically identified in the contract by name or description. On incorporation, the company will have the same rights and remedies under the contract as if it had been a party to the contract.

Statutory references

Arbitration Acts 1950, 1975 and 1979
Business Names Act 1985
Companies Act 1975
Company Law Reform Bill
Contracts (Rights of Third Parties) Act 1999
European Communities Act 1972
Income and Corporation Taxes Act 1970 (as amended)
Limited Liability Partnership Act 2000
Limited Partnership Act 1907
Partnership Act 1890
Registration of Business Names Act 1916

3

Money

What you put in the business and what you take out are basic. The sole trader's and partner's freedom to choose their route to profit is counterbalanced by their exposure to personal unlimited liability for business debts, but the directors and management of limited companies are to a large extent protected by the companies legislation.

Sole trader

Business capital is the cash and assets which you put into the business and extra capital can only be raised by way of a loan. Financial commitment is total and takings should not be seen as personal income but as interest-free working and growth capital for the business.

Partnership

Partners are in a similar situation to sole traders but the partners can agree that interest is paid on loans to the business. Failing agreement, there is a 5 per cent limit on advances exceeding initial contributions, unless a different rate can be implied from the custom of the trade or the course of dealing between the partners.

The partnership agreement should therefore specify an annual rate of interest payable on capital from time to time standing to the partners' credit.

The amount should be stated to be an outgoing, and deducted and paid as a business expense before profits and profit shares are calculated.

Certain loans of more than £25,000 including the cost of the credit must comply with the Consumer Credit Act 1974 (see Chapter 9).

You can raise outside capital by taking in a limited partner, whose liability is limited to the amount of the loan. No control is lost because involvement in the business imposes full liability on the limited partner.

Depending on your asset position and profit record additional capital can also be raised at interest and/or on security.

One partner's signature is acceptable in most transactions but your agreement should specify the amount and the kind of transaction which partners can complete on behalf of the business. Loans secured by a charge or mortgage should be approved by all the partners.

Partnership profits

Unless specified in the agreement:

- profits less expenses are business receipts without taking into account work in progress, stock in trade and book debts;
- profits are divided equally;
- partners cannot draw for current expenses against future profits;
- increases in goodwill are not taken into account.

The agreement should therefore make appropriate provision for the above in the annual accounts.

Corporate capital

A company's capital structure is more complicated. If two directors each contribute £300 to form a company with a nominal or authorised capital of £1,000, each taking £50 shares with a par (or nominal) value of £10 per share, or the sole director of a single-member company puts up £600, taking up 100 shares with a par value of £10 per share, the £600 is the company's *paid-up capital*. The £1,000 is the *nominal capital*, that is, the maximum share capital which the Memorandum authorises the company to issue. The balance of £400 is *uncalled capital*. The company can call on this at any time, in accordance with the Articles, unless it is agreed to make all or part *reserve capital* which is only called on in a liquidation. Companies will no longer have to fix their nominal/authorised capital when the Company Law Reform Bill comes into force.

References to share capital on letterheads and documents must be to paid-up capital. This fixes the minimum value of the net assets which must be raised initially and as far as possible maintained in the business, but usually has no relationship to the value of company assets or the market value of the shares. To see if a company is undercapitalised you must look at the balance sheet.

Corporate profits

Payment for shares can be in cash or in kind, including goodwill, know-how or an undertaking for work or services. The contribution of capital gives a right to a share of distributed profits but does not necessarily fix the proportion to which the contributor is entitled.

Rights attached to shares, including the right to vote and receive dividends, depend on the Memorandum, Articles, and shareholders' agreement, if any. Control is retained if you hold 75 per cent of the voting shares.

Most rights can be varied with the consent of three-quarters of the shareholders affected, by their extraordinary resolution or in accordance with a clause in the Memorandum or Articles. Thereafter, changes can only be made by consent and class rights stated to be unalterable in the Memorandum can only be varied with the consent of all the shareholders or by a scheme of arrangement.

Preference shares have a preference over other shares in repayment of capital and/or dividends which are paid at a fixed percentage rate before ordinary dividends. Unless otherwise stated, dividends are cumulative. Arrears must therefore be paid before ordinary dividends but non-cumulative dividends are lost if not paid when due.

Redeemable preference shares are more like debentures which are dealt with below.

Share warrants, with or without voting rights, are usually issued only to fully paid-up shareholders although they are sometimes attached to debentures with an option for future conversion to fully paid-up shares. They are negotiable and, if lost, the holder may lose dividends which are usually paid when the coupon attached to the warrant is sent to the company.

Increasing the company's capital

Restrictions on providing financial assistance to potential or actual share-holders to acquire or purchase the company's shares are to be abolished and it will be easier to make capital reductions when the Company Law Reform Bill comes into force. Until then increases in capital permitted by the Memorandum must also comply with the Articles but both Memorandum and Articles can, if necessary, be changed to permit an increase.

The Registrar must be notified of increases in capital within 15 days of the passing of the enabling resolution, sent a copy of the resolution and, if changed, copies of the amended Memorandum and/or Article.

Shareholders have pre-emptive rights to new issues in proportion to existing holdings, unless this is excluded by the Articles, payment is not in cash, there is a fixed dividend or the directors are authorised to allot shares.

The directors' conditional or unconditional authority to allot shares for a fixed or indefinite period must be included in the Articles or granted by shareholders, who can revoke or vary the authority. If for a fixed period, the expiry date must be stated.

Variation of existing shareholders' rights should be through a scheme of arrangement agreed by a majority of shareholders in number, holding at least three-quarters of the shares. The scheme must be approved by the court.

Shares cannot be issued at less than par value. If new shares are issued at over par value, the premium must be transferred to a share premium account. This is part of the company's capital and can only be distributed with the consent of the court unless used for a bonus or rights issue, as a premium for redemption of redeemable preference shares or debentures, or to write off the expense of another issue.

Reducing the company's capital

The company can reduce its capital by buying back shares. Transactions in small family-run companies are treated as straightforward sales of shares. The only tax payable is capital gains tax but there are heavy penalties if you make mistakes and expert advice should be sought before taking action.

Loans

Some loans and credit facilities of under £25,000, including the cost of the credit, must comply with the Consumer Credit Act 1974 (see page 149).

Companies

Special provisions apply to loans and lending facilities extended to directors and their 'connections'. Loans, guarantees and security of up to £10,000 can be extended to directors and connected persons, if made in the ordinary course of business and on the same basis as would apply to someone of the same financial standing as the borrower.

Connected persons are: a director's (business) partner, spouse, child and step-child, companies with which the director is associated and of which he or she controls at least a fifth of the votes at general meetings, a trustee of any trust of which he or she, the family group or associated company is a beneficiary, and the business partner of a connected person.

An advance of up to £20,000 can be made to directors for properly incurred business expenses, with the shareholders' prior consent given in general meeting. If they do not give their approval at or before the next annual general meeting, the transaction is conditional on the loan being repaid, or any other liability relating to the transaction being discharged, within six months of that meeting.

Unlimited loans can be made to directors if made in the ordinary course of business and available on the same terms to outsiders, or the company is in the lending field.

Money-lending companies which ordinarily provide such loans to employees can lend up to £100,000 to directors to buy or improve their only or main residence for tax purposes. This is, however, a maximum from which must be deducted other cash or credit facilities already provided. Such companies can also make loans or quasi-loans (undertakings to reimburse a creditor) and extend guarantees to directors and connected persons if they provide the same facilities to outsiders.

Non-cash assets valued over £2,000 or equal to 10 per cent of the company's called-up capital cannot be handed to directors, shadow directors or their connections, or acquired by the company without the shareholders' consent either before, or within a reasonable period after, the transaction. If annual accounts comply with the Companies Act, the limit is £100,000 or 10 per cent of the company's net assets as stated in the most recent accounts.

'Quasi-loans' – where the company undertakes to reimburse a director or connected person's creditor – of up to £5,000 are permitted if repayable within two months. The company can also enter into credit transactions with, or on behalf of, directors or persons connected with them, of up to £10,000.

Credit facilities and arrangements and the provision of guarantees and security to directors and their connections must be disclosed in the annual accounts, or the directors' reports, unless the company's contingent net liability does not exceed £10,000. Other transactions with directors and their connections must be included in the accounts unless the net value does not exceed £2,000 or 1 per cent of the net value of the company's assets to a maximum of £10,000.

There is no top limit on loans to employees to buy company shares or to set up a trust to buy shares for employees, including full-time salaried directors.

The company can assist anyone to buy its shares, provided its assets are not thereby reduced or, if reduced, the loan comes from distributable profits. The assistance can be by way of gift, loan, guarantee, security, indemnity or any other financial help and must be given in good faith and in the company's interests and with the shareholders' consent. The directors must also make a statutory declaration setting out details of the transaction and their opinion as to the financial viability of the company and the auditors must state whether the directors' opinion is reasonable.

Fines and penalties

Transactions made in contravention of the legislation may be cancelled and repayment or restitution ordered by the court.

Dividends

Dividends must come from profits, not capital. Profits mean accumulated realised profits after account has been taken of depreciation, not previously used for distribution or capitalisation, from which is deducted accumulated realised losses not previously written off.

Dividend declarations are self-contained, so previous losses need not be set against profits and losses, nor do losses on fixed capital have to be made good before profits are ascertained, but you must make up losses of circulating capital.

Loans to companies and LLPs

Trading businesses can borrow and give security without specific provision in the Memorandum and Articles or partnership agreement but both the Memorandum and Articles or the partnership agreement should give the company and its directors or the designated partners the widest possible powers.

Additional capital can be raised by issuing debentures. These can be in a series with similar rights attached or one of a class when the debenture can be transferable or negotiable.

Debentures secured on specific assets are fixed charges. Charges over all business assets, including stock in trade, goodwill and so on, are floating charges. This type of charge permits free dealing with the assets but the charge automatically becomes fixed if the business is wound up or stops trading, or is in default of the terms of the loan and the debenture-holder proceeds to enforce the security. Separate fixed and floating charges can be created but the floating charge is always enforceable after the fixed charge, whenever made, unless the fixed charge prohibits a loan with prior rights and the lender under the fixed charge knows of the restriction.

The 1989 Companies Act lists the kind of charges which must be registered at Companies House and the Registrar must be notified of repayment. If not registered, debts are valid but only as unsecured debts. Fixed charges on registered land must also be registered under the Land Registration Act 2002 and on unregistered land under the Land Charges Act 1972.

Companies and LLPs must keep their own register of charges at the registered office which must be available for public inspection. Copies of the charges must also be available at the registered office for inspection by creditors and shareholders or partners.

If the company or LLP is jointly liable with an individual and the loan falls within the Consumer Credit Act 1974, the loan must comply with the Act.

Both companies and LLPs must produce a certificate under the Companies Act as proof the charge has been registered.

Statutory references

Companies Acts 1985 and 1989
Consumer Credit Act 1974
Finance Act 1982
Income and Corporation Taxes Act 1970 (as amended)
Insolvency Act (No 2) 1994
Land Charges Act 1972
Land Registration Act 2002
Limited Liability Partnership Act 2000
Limited Partnership Act 1907
Partnership Act 1890

Choosing a Solicitor

Yolanda Dolling – consultant to **LawyerLocator.co.uk**

Although timely legal advice to help get fundamentals like employee contracts right is a far healthier option than damage limitation, the tendency is to look for a solicitor only when the storm clouds loom. Under pressure it is hard to make the wisest choices. The purpose of this chapter is to provide some simple guidelines for choosing the right adviser for you and working as an effective team.

Solicitor or barrister?

In England and Wales the legal profession consists of solicitors and barristers. The distinction is similar to the difference between a medical GP and a hospital consultant. Solicitors are invariably the first port of call.

Since 2004, barristers have been able to accept instructions direct from the public without having to go through a solicitor, provided that the barrister has three years post training experience, has completed a 'public access' training course and has the appropriate insurance. Instructing a barrister directly might be a smart move where you need expert advice on a specific area of law or need documents drafted for you to use, but there are legal restrictions on the type of matter in which a barrister can act for you directly. For example, barristers are not allowed to act directly in most areas of criminal, family and immigration work and although they may draft a document or letter for you they cannot send it on headed notepaper on your behalf. If a barrister is unable to act on your behalf because of any restrictions he will advise you to instruct a solicitor.

What type of solicitor do you need?

You need a solicitor to whom you are able to explain your needs. A solicitor should be committed to attaining your realistic chosen goals, advise you on the best course of action within an agreed budget and demonstrate through his or her experience that they can meet those objectives. Most solicitors specialise in areas of law in which they have had the most experience and it is essential that you locate the expert in the field of law in which you need advice. They usually work in partnership, covering many different areas of specialisation within a single practice. However, smaller firms, including sole practitioners, may well be capable of providing the effective and professional service you need. They may also be located in your vicinity which can be an advantage.

Where do I look?

- Ask colleagues and friends for recommendations.
- Talk to trade associations, chambers of commerce and professional bodies.
- Look at the law practices in your vicinity.

It is hard to beat recommendations from people that you trust, and checking that referrals really suit your needs has become a lot easier in the internet age. Many law firms have their own websites where you can confirm that their experience meets your needs before you pick up the phone. Similarly, experts in a particular field of law are now easy to identify online. An authoritative directory of solicitors and law firms like LawyerLocator.co.uk will, in seconds, find the specialists in your town or post code, throughout the United Kingdom.

In 2007 the Legal Services Bill will complete its passage through Parliament and is widely expected to shake up the profession. For the first time, other companies such as banks, insurance companies and supermarkets will be allowed to invest in law firms by becoming partners in 'alternative business structures.' This is intended to make the market for the provision of legal services more competitive by providing more choice to consumers and small businesses, leading to a better and more efficient service for all.

Do you really need a solicitor – couldn't you handle this yourself?

You usually know instinctively if you are facing an issue that you can deal with on your own. A late payment penalty is one thing, but a potential prosecution for breaking the Trade Descriptions Act is another. What you need to ascertain is simply: how serious is this and who must you see to evaluate the situation fully? If in doubt, always seek professional help.

What are you seeking to achieve?

Identifying your aims at an early stage will help you find the right adviser and him or her to achieve your goals. Be realistic in your expectations. For instance you may want to consider an out of court settlement. This is likely to save you valuable time, not to mention anxiety (given the inherent uncertainty of litigation) and expense. However, compromise is not always possible or appropriate. An experienced solicitor will help you evaluate your situation and provide a balanced view of likely outcomes.

Can I afford it? What do solicitors charge?

Solicitors may charge an agreed price for an assignment, but their basis of charges will be confirmed in writing at the outset in their Client Care Letter to you. This will detail likely charges (also called "profit costs"), any VAT and anticipated expenses (called "disbursements"). However, most solicitors charge by the hour for time they spend on your case. They must justify the work they carry out as being relevant and reasonable. They must keep accurate and verifiable time records.

From the very outset, solicitors must estimate your likely charges and keep you informed of any changes in that estimate. The Client Care Letter also explains how and when bills are delivered. Staged payments to cover costs or disbursements are often made during the course of litigation cases. The Client Care Letter will also deal with complaints procedures.

If you win a civil court case you may recover some or most of your legal costs from the other party. This is always at the judge's discretion, but the Court rules provide that the successful party usually recovers costs from the loser. However, this is based on a Court regulated scale which in reality means that you will recover around 60-70 per cent of the costs you have incurred. Remember, always think at the start of any case: does the defendant have the resources to pay your claim and the costs? If you are in doubt it may be wiser not to embark on the exercise.

In all cases a sensible client must balance the likely expense against the benefits to be achieved or the harm to be prevented.

Preparing for the first meeting and what to ask

Having found your solicitor, ensure that your time with them is effective and productive. Find out what you can about the firm and the lawyer with whom you will be dealing as soon as possible:

- How long have they been established?
- Have they experience in the area you need advice on?
- Can they provide client references?
- Have they had cases reported in the legal press?

The firm's own website may answer many such questions.

A solicitor or barrister has a duty to provide you with an estimate of costs and disbursements and it is common to provide a ceiling over which he will not go without further instruction. However, you should make sure that the cash-flow consequences to the business of pursuing a legal matter are addressed.

Bring all the documents (emails, contracts, receipts etc) concerning the case to the first meeting, however irrelevant you may consider them to be. If they are bulky, ask the solicitor to come to you. In any case, they may need to visit you.

If, for example you have agreed to sell your business, your solicitor will need to know about every aspect of the business: customers, staff, service contracts, debts, liabilities and assets. If you are a director and shareholder, you will be required to warrant formally that the assets being sold do exist and that nothing to diminish their value is known to you. The purchaser must know exactly what they are buying. Any failure to make full and candid disclosure may result in liabilities being claimed under the warranties you have to give. In all cases, identify in your mind what you are seeking to achieve. Then ask your solicitor whether he or she agrees that this is achievable. It is always a good idea to discuss with your solicitor the outcome of similar cases they have handled in the past to allow you to understand what the best and worst case outcomes might be. Ensure your potential liability for costs is made clear. If you lose the case, you are likely to have to meet your own legal costs as well those of the successful party.

After your initial meeting, consider if the necessary rapport and trust has been established. Ask yourself if you feel comfortable and confident with this person.

You may wish to speak to other clients who have used them previously, or other partners in the firm. If you are still unsure, perhaps you ought to consider another solicitor.

The duties of a solicitor

Every solicitor is bound by the terms of the contract with a client and the wider duty of care under general law. All solicitors also adhere to the regulations and professional standards imposed by the solicitors' professional body, The Law Society. Complaints against solicitors are now handled by the Consumer Complaints Service who will work with you to find the best solution for your complaint. Every firm also has its own internal complaints procedures which should be followed initially and most issues can be resolved in this way.

Where any client considers that a solicitor has not acted competently, or has been negligent, a court action may be considered. Every solicitor must hold substantial Professional Indemnity Insurance to meet such claims. The minimum level of cover to meet such claims is usually in excess of £1 million and larger firms cover substantially in excess of that sum.

Duty of confidence

Every solicitor has a duty to hold in strict confidence everything said by a client. This duty continues even after the relationship with the solicitor has ended. However, this strict rule is governed by certain legislation where in a few and very special circumstances - for instance money laundering investigations – the duty is overridden by the requirements of disclosure.

Notes

The author *Yolanda Dolling was responsible for establishing **LawyerLocator.co.uk**, and is now a consultant in the legal and professional services sector.*

__LawyerLocator.co.uk__ is an online directory containing details of over 12,000 law firms and 45,000 solicitors nationwide, providing public access to law firm credentials free of charge. It is owned by LexisNexis Butterworths who also publish the Butterworths Law Directory, a primary resource for the legal profession from which the data on LawyerLocator is derived.

LexisNexis®
Butterworths

4

Running the business

Sole traders are restricted only by access to capital and their ability to generate profits. Partners and directors share the load but their agreement and cooperation is vital to business success and you may be liable for their incompetence or dishonesty.

Partners' responsibilities

Partners act on behalf of the partnership and their partners. The law implies that they deal with one another fairly and in good faith.

You must therefore account to the business for profits and monies made on business assets and you are liable for any shortfall in payments made by other partners unless the transaction is their personal responsibility. Whatever the partnership agreement states, outsiders can assume partners act for the partnership unless they are informed to the contrary or the transaction is outside the partnership's usual business.

If you do not make specific provision in the agreement the following applies:

- All partners in a trading business can borrow on security and draw, sign, accept and negotiate negotiable instruments; in any other business, they can only draw and endorse ordinary cheques.
- All partners take part in management. If they do not work full time in the business, the partnership can be dissolved – the agreement

could permit partners to go into business on their own account, provided they are not in competition with the partnership.

■ Decisions are by partners' majority vote – the agreement could therefore have an arbitration clause so decisions can go to arbitration rather than the courts.

■ Profits and losses are divided equally – the agreement should therefore make provision for sharing profits, and paying salaries and interest on capital contributions.

■ The agreement should state whether business assets are owned wholly or partly by a partner or the partnership. If the partnership is a partner's tenant and this is not in the agreement, the partnership can only be evicted if the partnership is dissolved. Assets acquired after you start trading belong to the partnership if purchased for business use or on its account but land is a special case. It is classified as 'personal property', not real estate; thus it is considered as a cash sum and must be sold if a partner dies or the partnership is dissolved.

The members (partners) of limited liability partnerships (LLPs) must sign and file the partnership's annual accounts at Companies House and notify it of changes in membership, changes in members' names and addresses, and any change to the Registered Office address.

Third parties will usually contract directly with the LLP which, like a company, is a separate legal entity. The partners are therefore protected by limited liability although individual partners are liable for fraud and may be liable in negligence.

LLPs: designated members' responsibilities

Designated members have the same rights as the other partners but they have in addition a duty to:

■ appoint auditors (if required);
■ sign the accounts on behalf of the members;

- deliver the accounts to the Registrar;
- notify the Registrar of changes of members and their details, changes to the registered office address or the LLP's name;
- prepare, sign and deliver the annual return to the Registrar;
- act on the LLP's behalf if it is wound up and dissolved.

The partners can decide at any time to appoint any member a designated member on notice delivered to the Registrar, and designated members can resign from office with the agreement of the other members any time after incorporation, but they must inform the Registrar within 14 days of the change.

Directors' responsibilities

Whatever the title, a director is anyone occupying the position of a director and anyone in accordance with whose directions the directors are accustomed to act – other than professional advisers. Directors aged under 16 cannot be registered in Scotland. There is no minimum or maximum age in England and Wales but the young director must be able to sign the consent to act and you should take legal advice if you want to appoint someone very young. Some foreign nationals are excluded, so check with the Home Office Immigration and Nationality Directorate, Lunar House, Wellesley Road, Croydon CR9 2BY (Tel: 0845 010 5200) or their website www.ind.homeoffice.gov.uk before appointing a non-British director. Directors are bound by the powers given by the Memorandum and Articles and their responsibility is to the company, not individual shareholders. They must act honestly and in the company's best interests.

Directors are not responsible for their co-directors' dishonesty. They and management are, however, personally liable to outsiders, the company and shareholders for dishonesty and negligence and for anything done without reference to the company – for instance, placing orders without referring to the company or paying by cheque not properly made out in the company's name. They are also liable for acts done outside the powers set out in the Memorandum and Articles but they are only liable to outsiders if the outsider dealt with them in good faith and the shareholders have not ratified the transaction. If the shareholders refuse approval, the company can also demand reimbursement.

Executive and non-executive directors have the same liability, but only if they are negligent or dishonest and intend to act fraudulently is there a liability for consequential loss caused to the company. Active involvement in a company carrying on business for a fraudulent purpose and continuing to trade when there is no reasonable prospect of creditors being paid can bring a personal liability without limit for all the company's debts and, in addition, a fine and/or imprisonment. Directors' general duties, modified to reflect modern business practice, are specified under the Company Law Reform Bill.

The directors and the company have responsibilities under the employment, industrial training and health and safety legislation and they can be convicted of crimes – for instance, offences under the Road Traffic Acts. The directors are also liable for deficits in the employer's slice of employees' National Insurance contributions and VAT. Directors are required to take note of employees' as well as shareholders' interests but they must also have regard to the best interests of the company.

Directors' service contracts for over 12 months must be available for shareholders' inspection at the registered office or principal place of business. Contracts exceeding five years must be approved by shareholders and if there is no written contract the company must record a memorandum or note of the agreed terms. If you have not changed the standard Articles or there is no special provision in the service contract, a director can be removed from office by shareholders' majority vote and entitlement to compensation depends on the contract. Directors must give written notice of resignation and appointments of successors must be confirmed by the shareholders. The Articles usually provide for a third of the directors to retire each year in rotation but they can be immediately re-elected and a managing director can only be appointed if permitted by the Articles.

Details of directors' share and debenture dealings must be given to the company within five days of the transaction.

The Registrar must be kept informed of the names of the directors and where contracts, memoranda and copies are kept.

THE CHARTERED QUALITY INSTITUTE

CQI company membership **provides the resource to support your employee performance and business excellence.**

If you want to tell your customers, suppliers, staff and stakeholders that quality is at the heart of everything you do, become a company member.

Membership
- FREE CQI individual membership (ACQI)

Learning
- one-day training on business quality management
- exclusive discounts on CQI training courses

Networking
- exclusive discounts for members on learning and networking events
- FREE membership of the CQI's eleven special interest groups - specific industry sectors

Resources
- receive *Qualityworld*, the UK's leading quality magazine, and our other regular publications
- the CQI 'Commitment to Quality' logo to print on your stationery and website

Consultancy
- access to our Management Consultants Register, a network of high quality consultants

Through innovation and care we create quality

Contact the CQI for a free membership pack on
T: +44 (0)20 7245 6722 or
E: membership@thecqi.org
www.thecqi.org

Chartered Quality Institute

Sunday Times

The Chartered Quality Institute became a reality on 18 January 2007, born out of its well known predecessor the Institute of Quality Assurance. Based in London, but with a full national network of branches and regions, its reason for existence is to educate and train individuals to understand and operate the wide range of business improvement methodologies that now exist. Some familiar names for these methodologies include ISO 9000, the BQF Excellence Model, Six Sigma, LEAN and Balanced Scorecard.

Recognition of the qualification that gives CQI members their professional status is through the grant of corporate membership and the right to use the post nominal letters MCQI. However, the stepping stone, non-voting grade of Associate of the CQI (ACQI) confers all the benefits of membership and is a way of recognising those who have embarked on the quality journey, even at its very beginning. More importantly, it provides them with access to the information they need not only to progress their professional careers, but also to add value in the workplace. Gavin Johns said of his membership as an Associate: *"The main reason why I joined the Institute: learning. Through the Institute and the University of Northampton, over a six year period, the various Diploma modules enabled me to enhance my knowledge of quality. I was able to apply this knowledge through leadership as a Manager of Quality at my company."*

At a similar grade, Iwona Polony, a relatively recent arrival into the country, said of the CQI's predecessor, the IQA: *"Through its people and on going contact with its members I've grown and developed as an individual and as a professional. The IQA has made a great impact on my life and had a large part to play in my decision to pursue a career in Quality management."*

The CQI has always been conscious of the need to involve itself in the small and medium business sectors, for here really lies the heart of British Industry. It was instrumental in producing a small business standard to help businesses start their own quality journey without fuss and without expense. It is free and can be downloaded from the web together with its excel based self-assessment tool and you will find both on **www.thecqi.org/mcr/smallbusinessstandard.shtml**. Progression from that can be achieved by attending any of the relevant CQI courses, and conscious that time spent away from a business is often business lost there are a range of short courses which can help add value and improve competitive edge. The discounts on these for members are a generous ten or fifteen percent and soon eat a large hole in the amount spent on membership. And if there are a number of people requiring training in, say, a medium sized company or group of companies it is often better to have the CQI run a course on your own premises with costs negotiated individually on a case by case basis. Concessions are worth having if your company has joined the Company Membership scheme and will go a long way to meeting the costs of membership, if not covering it completely.

The CQI is taking quality into the information age. Conscious that the face of business is changing and that more and more electronic means of communication, both internal and external, are dominating lives and the conduct of business, it has sought to derive a new message for the promotion of quality, to stress its importance and its values both to business and the individual. And neither is it tied, as used to be the case, to manufacturing; quality affects us all and is all our business. Indeed, the CQI's Company Membership scheme is designed to demonstrate a commitment to quality across the entire range of businesses and offer a full range of appropriate benefits. As witness to this here are the views of just one company, again referring to the CQI's previous guise:

"As a small market research agency, we gain two main benefits from being a Company Member…

    1. Inside track on quality issues currently being discussed

    2. The ability to promote/demonstrate our commitment to quality to clients and prospective clients, by mentioning our membership of the Institute

The fact that the market research industry already has clear and widely accepted quality standards (eg BS7911 and MRQSA) also makes our link to the IQA relevant and topical."

The key to pursing a quality agenda, improving the way business is done and achieving excellence in product and service is through innovation. Through the lateral thinking of managers at every level, and this is key, improvements in products and services and in delivery systems will lead to improved business and greater stakeholder satisfaction. If the care required to make innovation successful is then applied, then quality shines through. This is care about our society, care about our profession, care for the environment and a passion for quality – and caring in general. This leads as well to improved business and leads inevitably to increased stakeholder satisfaction.

Quality is achieved through innovation and care and is the way to improve and sustain business into the information age. But what is this information age and how does it affect us? Because affect us it does – big and small alike. If someone can buy what they want from their armchair, and cheaper than going to a local shop, then we all lose, and on grounds of cost and convenience many will take that route. The only way to win in the face of this competition is to win on quality. Quality of product and quality of delivery, by taking an innovative and caring approach. As Richard Lambert, the Director General of the CBI said, on hearing of the grant of the charter: *"The UK is facing a challenging era of change and we must make the best of the opportunities arising from globalisation. We can't compete with emerging economies on price. The way ahead for Britain is to create added value, quality branded goods and services. As it approaches its 90th birthday, the IQA has deservedly been awarded a Royal Charter, which rightly recognizes not only its dedication to raising the profile of quality over this period but also its role in promoting such a vital component of the UK's future global success."*

His views were echoed by Sir Richard Branson who offered the opinion that: *"...the 21st Century, which will be the one where product and service will demonstrate survival in a totally globalised economy…and even in space for that matter!"*

There is also the question of cycle time. With computer aided design and rapid communication the opportunities are there for the entrepreneur to carve inside the opposition's cycle time and beat them to market with a new way of conducting business or delivering a product or service. Then there is the issue of connectivity. This has two facets to it – on the one hand it is a fabulous asset for moving ideas around, for creating and sustaining partnerships and for working together generally. On the other hand email means that your failure to deliver can be public knowledge within minutes.

And we must adapt our working practices to meet the challenges this offers if we are to compete and survive.

So what does the charter mean to the CQI and to business? For the CQI it is recognition of the furrow they ploughed for so long as the IQA; it is recognition that they truly represent a profession, the Quality profession; and it is recognition that the government acknowledges that what they do and they way in which they do it is in the public interest. For business it presents the opportunity to use the CQI to improve the way things are done, to perpetually improve and to survive in an increasingly hostile world, to place quality at the top of the boardroom agenda and to *place quality at the heart of their organisation.*

If you want to know more about how the Chartered Quality Institute can help your business or organisation then contact Frank Steer, the Chief Executive, on **fsteer@thecqi.org** and for the detail of services Virginia Corbett on **vcorbett@thecqi.org** or Will Matthewman on **wmatthewman@thecqi.org** They can all be reached on **0207 245 6722**.

The company secretary

The company must have a company secretary who can also be a director – although not the sole director – but who cannot then sign documents in both capacities. The secretary's liability is similar to a director's but involvement is often confined to administration, including ensuring documents and returns are sent to the Registrar and that proper company registers are kept. The secretary cannot therefore commit the company in business transactions unless authorised by the Board.

When the Company Law Reform Bill comes into force companies will not be required to have a company secretary but someone will of course have to take over the company secretary's administrative responsibilities.

Single-member companies

The single-shareholder company must also have at least one director and a secretary who cannot be the sole director. The single shareholder, in person or by proxy, is a quorum for meetings whatever is stated in the Articles and 'meetings' must be minuted and decisions formally notified to the company, unless made by written resolution.

Details of unwritten contracts between the company and the single shareholder/director must be set out in a memorandum or recorded in the minutes of the next directors' meeting, unless the contract is made in the ordinary course of the company's business.

Auditors

The company must appoint and re-appoint auditors at the annual general meeting, unless the requirement has been dispensed with (see page 57). They are then appointed at least 28 days before the day on which copies of the previous year's accounts are circulated, unless they have been required to put them before the general meeting.

The LLP's designated members must appoint the first auditors before the end of the first financial year; thereafter they must be appointed or reappointed annually within two months of approval of the previous year's accounts.

Accounts

The only purpose of accounts for the *sole trader* and *ordinary partnerships* is to record receipts and payments, profits and losses, and to chart business progress. Annual accounts are then drawn up showing assets and liabilities and, for the partnership, what is due to each partner. Partners must have access to the books but they are not available to anyone else except the inspector of taxes and the VAT inspector.

Businesses with a turnover of under £15,000 can submit simplified three-line accounts to the Revenue showing only annual turnover, total purchases, expenses and the resulting net profit.

'Small' LLPs and companies with a turnover of up to £5.6 million and/or with a balance sheet total of not more than £2.8 million and/or with an average of no more than 50 employees may file Abbreviated Accounts. Two out of three of the criteria categorise the LLP or company and current and preceding years must be taken into account when deciding if the business is 'small'.

You do not have to include the full balance sheet, profit and loss account and designated partners' or directors' report but must file:

- ■ a short version of the balance sheet with aggregated amounts for each item except debtors and creditors *and* notes explaining how the figures are made up;
- ■ a special auditor's report – unless you are also claiming audit exemption (see page 54).

The balance sheet must include a statement that the accounts are prepared in accordance with Part VII of the Companies Act 1985 relating to small LLPs and companies *and* the auditor's report must state that in the auditor's opinion you are entitled to submit abbreviated accounts.

The accounting reference period (ARP) – the date for the LLP or company's financial year – is fixed according to the accounting reference date (ARD). The first ARP must be between 6 and 18 months, beginning with the date of incorporation. Subsequent ARPs are for 12 months. The ARD is fixed at any time within nine months of incorporation by notice given to the Registrar. If none is fixed, the ARD is the last day of the month in which the anniversary of incorporation falls. Copies of the Accounts must be sent to the Registrar within 22 months of incorporation and thereafter within 10 months of the ARP.

Copies of the full accounts – that is, the balance sheet, profit and loss account, auditor's report and the designated partners' or directors' report must be sent to partners or share- and debenture-holders 21 days before the partners' or shareholders' meetings and to anyone entitled to receive notice of the meetings. They can be sent summary instead of full financial statements if the accounts are audited. Partners or share- and debenture-holders must also receive copies of the last accounts. The accounts can now be prepared in compliance with the accounting requirements of the Limited Liability Partnership Act or Companies Acts (UK GAAP) or the EEC's International Accounting Standards (IAS).

The designated partners or directors are responsible for preparing the annual accounts and for filing them with the Registrar within the required time limits. They are liable to fines and/or imprisonment for accounts that do not comply with the Acts and late filing. Persistent offenders may face disqualification from acting as designated partners or directors for up to 15 years.

LLP and company records must comply with the Limited Liability Partnership and Companies Acts and be specific. They must explain transactions and disclose the financial position of the business with reasonable accuracy. Daily receipts and expenses, sales and purchases and details of stock, assets and liabilities must be recorded. Records must be kept for three years and books must be available at the registered office or other place designated by the partners or directors.

Exemption from audit for small LLPs and companies

Small LLPs and companies entitled to file abbreviated accounts can file unaudited accounts.

The balance sheet must include a statement by the designated partners or directors that:

- the partnership or company was entitled to the exemption;
- they acknowledge responsibility for ensuring the LLP or company keeps accounting records in compliance with the Limited Liability Partnership or Companies Acts and for preparing accounts giving a true and fair view of the LLP or company's affairs;
- advantage has been taken of the exemption for individual accounts;
- in their opinion the LLP or company is entitled to take advantage of the exemption;
- the accounts have been prepared in accordance with Part VII of the Limited Liability Partnership of Companies Act 1985.

And in the case of a company:

- the shareholders have not demanded an audit.

The LLP agreement or Articles must permit use of the exemption but company shareholders with at least 10 per cent of the company's issued capital or of any class of shares can demand an audit on at least a month's notice to the company's registered office given before the end of the financial year.

And it should be borne in mind that banks and credit managers rely on financial information to assess creditworthiness and like to have the reassurance of an independent audit.

The audit exemption for earlier years can be claimed if the accounts are approved by the board and delivered on time but they must then be accompanied by an independent auditor's report prepared by a qualified accountant, who need not be a registered auditor but must be a member of:

- The Institute of Chartered Accountants;
- The Association of Chartered Certified Accountants;
- The Association of Authorised Public Accountants;
- The Association of Accounting Technicians;
- The Association of International Accountants; or

■ The Chartered Institute of Management Accountants entitled to engage in public practice and independent of the company.

The same accountant can prepare the Accounts and make the report.

Some flat management companies may have to file audited accounts in compliance with the terms of their lease.

There are less stringent requirements for Accounts and audits under the Company Law Reform Bill, but you will have only 7 months after the year end to file annual reporting documents with the Registrar instead of 10 months.

Keeping the shareholders informed

The report, which must be signed by a director or the company secretary, must give a 'fair review of the development of the business... during the year and the position at the end of it' and include everything which materially affects the company, including details of:

- dividends, what is to be carried to reserve and retained for investment and bad debts;
- directors and their share- and debenture-holdings unless included in the notes to the accounts;
- directors' acquisition of company shares verified by the auditors;
- indemnities covering company officers;
- new share and debenture issues;
- the company's main activity and material changes in the company's business and asset position;
- important events affecting the company during the year, likely future developments and an outline of research and development activities;
- political and charitable gifts exceeding £200.

Meetings

LLPs are not required to have formal meetings or to make decisions by formal resolution.

Shareholders' meetings

Unless you have elected to dispense with meetings, companies must have an annual general meeting within 18 months of incorporation and once in every subsequent calendar year.

The annual general meeting considers the accounts and reports, approves dividends, elects directors and appoints, reappoints and agrees auditors' fees. Given the necessary majority of shareholders, the company can be forced to present a resolution for discussion at the annual general meeting. Otherwise, the directors or, depending on the Articles, two or more holders of more than a tenth of the fully paid-up voting shares can call an extraordinary general meeting to deal with other company business.

The auditors and shareholders must be notified of meetings and what is to be discussed in compliance with the Articles. Shareholders can speak and vote through a proxy. Notice is given when posted but the Articles should state that non-receipt will not invalidate meetings. Ninety-five per cent of the holders of voting shares can agree to dispense with notice and can agree not to meet at all, but dispensing with notice of the annual general meeting requires the consent of all shareholders with voting rights.

Resolutions are ordinary, special or extraordinary, depending on what is discussed. Ordinary and special resolutions are passed by a majority of those at the meeting and extraordinary resolutions need a three-quarters majority. Decisions are put to meetings by resolution and when passed bind the directors. Broadly, shareholders acting together can do anything permitted by the company's Memorandum and Articles unless it is prohibited by the Companies Acts, outsiders or creditors are affected or there is a public interest issue.

As an alternative and in spite of anything stated in the Memorandum and Articles, decisions can be made by written resolution, signed by all the shareholders entitled to vote, without serving notice of the contents and calling a meeting. The resolution must be minuted and the auditors must receive copies; the decision is only valid if they do not respond within seven days or they state it does not affect them as auditors or, if so, it does not require discussion at a shareholders' meeting.

This procedure enables the company, with the shareholders' consent, to dispense with some statutory requirements including having an annual general meeting, laying accounts before shareholders, voting to appoint auditors and extending the directors' indefinite authority (that is, beyond the five-year limit) to allot shares. Currently consent to the procedure must be obtained from all the shareholders.

The Company Law Reform Bill, however, does not require the company to hold meetings. Auditors and shareholders will still have to be notified about what is up for discussion but share- and debenture-holders will be able to make their decisions by written resolution and a simple or 75 per cent majority vote.

Anyone can chair meetings but the chairman of the board, if any, usually does so. Company business is, however, usually decided at board meetings. The board's powers depend on the Articles, but they can be delegated. Board meetings can be held anywhere and at any time but shareholders must be kept informed.

Minutes of meetings must be recorded in a Minute Book kept at the registered office and procedural points not included in, or prohibited by, the Memorandum and Articles can be written into the minutes. The decision who is to sign company cheques should be minuted unless the form of draft resolution sent by the company's bank is passed.

If management acts in good faith and in the company's interests, minority shareholders cannot interfere in the business. Shareholders can sue the company in their own name to protect individual rights but not to protect the company's interests, nor can they interfere with internal management. Otherwise only the company acting in general meeting can take legal action and the will of majority shareholders is therefore the will of the company. Shareholders, directors, personal representatives and liquidators can stop management acting illegally or beyond the powers given in the Memorandum and Articles or if the company's affairs are being conducted in a way which is, or will be, unfairly prejudicial to their interests. However, unless there is fraud or an unfair manipulation of the advantages of a majority holding or management is grossly negligent, the Memorandum and Articles can provide for ratification of almost anything by special or ordinary resolution.

A founding shareholder, one who has held shares for six months or has inherited the shares of a deceased shareholder, can ask the court to wind up the company on the ground that it is 'just and equitable' to do so. The order will only be made if there is no other remedy and the shareholder is not being unreasonable in insisting on a winding up.

As a last resort and only on substantial grounds, the Department of Trade and Industry can be called in to investigate the company but the complaining shareholders must lodge security for the costs of the investigation.

Statutory references

Business Names Act 1985
Civil Liability (Contribution) Act 1978
Companies Acts 1985 and 1989
Company Law Reform Bill
Company Directors Disqualification Act 1986
Industrial Training Act 1982
Insolvency Act 1986
Limited Liability Partnership Act 2000
Limited Partnership Act 1890
Registration of Business Names Act 1916
Road Traffic Act 1972
Transport Act 1968

5

Premises

You should seek legal and financial advice before investing in business premises and rent, which can be a substantial investment and a major part of your overheads.

Planning permission

Check whether current, proposed use or alterations are permitted by the local authority and/or local by-laws and if there have been complaints about use of the premises.

If you need consents it is worth making preliminary investigations yourself. You should also check whether you need anyone else's agreement including someone with an interest in the premises, such as the freeholder and lessees with tenancies with at least 10 years to run.

Some building does not require planning permission, including, subject to conditions, a 10 per cent addition to cubic content – not square footage. Some changes of use are also permitted, for instance from one shop to another. You need consent for 'material' change, demolition, most building works and 'material' widening of access to the highway, and sometimes for outside advertisements.

If the vendor has outline permission, check that time limits have not been exceeded – full, as opposed to outline, permission normally lasts for five years.

Unauthorised continuous use since the end of 1963 can be regularised with an established use certificate, otherwise it is unlawful. The occupier is liable for unlawful use and a vendor's undertaking, and indemnity for damages is no protection. Suing for misrepresentation and/or breach of covenant in a lease is expensive and of little value compared with the expense and impact of eviction without notice.

A recent decision under the Human Rights Act struck at the basis of this area of law, where many decisions are made by government. There is currently therefore a question mark over our planning law, and you should take expert advice before proceeding.

Leases

The landlord may have to consent to sale, alteration and/or change of use under an existing lease. Consent must be given within a reasonable time unless it is reasonable to withhold it and the landlord must serve written notice of the decision, specifying any conditions attached to the consent or the reasons for withholding it.

The landlord may have to consent to sale, alterations and/or change of use under an existing lease. Payment cannot be demanded from the incoming tenant, and if there are no structural alterations, the rent should not increase even if permitted by the lease. But the incoming tenant may have to undertake to reinstate premises if this is reasonable and pay for damage or diminution in value to the property or the landlord's adjoining property, as well as legal and other expenses.

The lease can prohibit change of use, alterations and improvements and the landlord can refuse consent unless the lease states consent cannot be 'unreasonably withheld'. Reasonable reasons must be given by the landlord; requiring more than the cost of actual compensation constitutes unreasonable refusal. The landlord cannot unreasonably withhold consent or impose unreasonable conditions if you make a written request to make reasonable alteration to the premises to accommodate disabled employees (see page 129).

An incoming tenant should ensure the vendor has a right to sell or sublet. Landlord and tenant can agree when the landlord can refuse to permit a sale of the lease, by for example forbidding a sale in the first or last three years of the term. They can also agree conditions, for example requiring an incoming tenant to give a personal guarantee. But if the landlord or a third party is unilaterally able to decide when and/or on what conditions you can sell, the terms of the lease must either require the decision to be reasonable or give you the right to have the matter independently decided. If this agreed term in the lease is worded inappropriately the landlord cannot unreasonably withhold consent, whatever the circumstances. If the sale requires the landlord's consent, a suitable tenant must be accepted, unless refusal is reasonable on grounds which would have been valid when the lease was created or it last changed hands. Payment for consent to sale or sublet can be demanded only if permitted by the lease. Consent must be given within a reasonable time unless it is reasonable to withhold it, and the landlord must serve written notice of the decision, specifying any conditions attached to the consent or the reasons for withholding it.

If, unknown to the purchaser, the vendor has no right to sell or sublet, the landlord must accept the purchaser and seek compensation from the vendor, but the purchaser may have to vacate if change of use is in breach of a superior lease or planning consent.

Leases granted for more than seven years must now be registered, otherwise the lease has no legal effect. Assignments of unregistered leases with more than seven years unexpired and the transfer of any registered lease, whatever its remaining length, must also be registered. Landlords consenting to assignment should require the assignee to register the lease, otherwise notices served by the landlord may not be effective. Leases of any length must also be registered if the lease does not commence until more than three months after the grant.

If the lease is for a fixed period or from year to year following a lease for a period of months or years, you can usually continue in occupation after expiry of the lease on the same terms. The Landlord and Tenant Act 1954 excludes some tenancies from the protection, including tenants living on the premises (who may be protected under the Rent Acts).

Renewal is subject to negotiation at the end of the tenancy and strict formalities and time limits apply. Usually the landlord must give between 6 and 12 months' notice, setting out the tenant's rights and stating whether he or she will oppose an application for a new tenancy. Otherwise the existing tenancy continues until the tenant asks for renewal.

The landlord's claim to possession must be on grounds contained in the 1954 Act, which are broadly similar to those in commercial leases, including delay in paying rent and failure to maintain, repair, use or manage the premises. The tenant must move if the landlord offers suitable alternative accommodation, the premises are to be let as part of a larger, more profitable unit or they are to be redeveloped or used by the landlord.

If negotiations break down, you can apply to the county court for a new lease. Again, there are time limits and whatever the stage of negotiations, apply to the court for a new tenancy two to four months after service of the landlord's notice of termination, otherwise you will lose your right to remain in occupation. The application should now be protected by notice under the Land Registration Act 2002.

If you go to court and the landlord cannot prove one of the statutory grounds, the court must grant a tenancy of up to 14 years on much the same terms as the old one, although rent is based on open market value.

If the only issue is the terms of the new lease, it may be cheaper and faster to use the Royal Institute of Chartered Surveyors (RICS) and Professional Arbitration on Court Terms (PACT) arbitration scheme.

If the landlord proves his case and you must move, you are entitled to *compensation for improvements*, provided you served three months' notice of your intention to do the work and there was no objection. If the landlord objected, you can apply to court for a certificate stating it was reasonable to do the work and again there are time limits.

Continuous occupation for 14 years entitles you to *compensation for disturbance* if the landlord is to let the premises as part of a larger unit or intends to redevelop or use them himself.

Outgoing tenants and their guarantors are now automatically released from the covenants when the lease is sold, but their involvement does not necessarily end. If the lease requires the landlord or anyone else to consent to the sale and also requires the outgoing tenant to guarantee the incoming tenant – under an 'authorised guarantee agreement' – the outgoing tenant or his guarantor can be called upon to remedy the incoming tenant's breach of certain covenants. If the outgoing tenant or guarantor then 'remedies the breach', for example by paying the amount or taking the action demanded by the landlord, either can claim a lease of the premises which overrides the incoming tenant's right to occupy.

NB: These provisions are fenced around with rules and regulations, requiring formal notices to be served on the various parties within specified time limits. Both tenants and landlord should therefore ensure they are fully informed as to the implications of the legislation.

Public access to the Land Registry

Documents held by the Land Registry are open to public inspection but the registrar has a discretion only to allow inspection of some documents, including leases and mortgages. You may want to apply for exemption for commercially or personally sensitive information, such as the identity of your guarantors.

Stamp duty land tax rates from 23 March 2006

Transfers of non-residential land and buildings

Rate	Total amount paid
Zero	£0 to £150,000
1%	Over £150,000 to £250,000
3%	Over £250,000 to £500,000
4%	Over £500,000

New non-residential leases – Duty on rent

Rate	Net present value of rent (NPV)
Zero	£0 to £150,000
1%	Over £150,000

The NPV calculation is reduced by £150,00 before applying the 1 per cent rate and duty on the premium is the same as for transfers of land but special rules apply if rent exceeds £600 pa.

Rent arrears

The landlord can seize the tenant's assets – levy distress – and sell them if rent is in arrear but only:

- ■ if the tenant has a continuing tenancy; or
- ■ if the tenancy has ended, during the six months after expiry;

and then only in daylight hours from Monday to Saturday inclusive. The right to levy distress is subject, and without prejudice, to the rights of prior creditors. If the landlord breaks the rules he is liable to damages.

NB: Landlord and tenant law is a technical area with infinite possibilities for expensive error, and before taking on a lease you should take legal advice.

Conditions of work

The Health and Safety at Work Act 1974 applies to premises where anyone is employed and covers employees, independent contractors, visitors, trespassers and the general public. You may also be held liable for damages.

The Act is primarily aimed at preventing accidents and imposing fines and penalties and both you and the business can be prosecuted. There is strict (automatic) liability for business activities which affect the health or safety of the public and if there is pollution the local authority can order works to be carried out or close you down. There is no time limit for prosecutions. Serious offences carry unlimited fines and up to two years' imprisonment and there is a continuing daily fine for some offences. It may therefore be helpful to consult the inspectorate and Employment Medical Advisory Service (EMAS) if business activities are likely to cause problems.

You must provide training and an appropriate working environment for disabled employees. This category includes employees suffering from HIV, multiple sclerosis and visual or other impairment. You must take reasonable steps to deal with physical features that act as a barrier to disabled people, taking into account cost and the size and type of the business. For instance, you may have to improve access to toilet and washing facilities, replace stairs with a ramp or provide more legible signs for employees with visual impairment.

Employees must work in reasonable safety and comfort, welfare and catering arrangements and toilet facilities must be clean and safe, and you are responsible for clothing left on the premises. Continuing instruction, information, training and supervision must be provided to protect employees' health and safety, particularly if they are inexperienced or have a poor command of English and they must use the protection and information provided.

Employees working with dangerous substances must be monitored and records kept for at least five years. If some dangerous substances are used, the employer must pay for employees to have regular health checks. Similar obligations apply to workers in the electrical industry.

Employers' liability to employees cannot be excluded or restricted for death or injury caused by defective plant, machinery, equipment or protective clothing and equipment. The liability cannot be delegated, unless it is reasonable to rely on expert advice or information or on the established practice of the trade. Both you and your employees are liable for non-compliance with the Management of Health and Safety at Work Regulations 1999; if you do not comply with the 1997 Fire Precautions (Workplace) Regulations your employees can claim compensation for consequential injury or illness. The Regulations are on HSE's website www.hse.gov.uk.

If employees are sent to someone else's premises, your responsibility is reduced to taking 'reasonable' care that they have a safe system of work and usually the responsibility then passes to the owner of the premises. Owners of machinery or equipment left on your premises are liable to anyone using it with their consent.

If you employ more than five people, *health, safety, welfare information and emergency safety procedures* must be displayed on the premises and rules about health and safety with details of management's and employees' responsibilities must be set out in a written statement which must be kept up to date. Employees who belong to a trade union can appoint a safety representative who must be consulted about your procedures and they can ask for a supervisory safety committee to be appointed. Drivers of vehicles carrying dangerous substances must be informed of the hazards involved and of emergency avoidance action. The information must be displayed in the cab of the vehicle.

Codes of practice covering health and safety procedures are available from The Stationery Office. It is a defence to show that you took all reasonable precautions and exercised due diligence. Accordingly, although non-compliance is not an offence, it can be persuasive evidence against you.

If you manufacture, supply or import goods, plant and machinery, systems of work and methods of handling, storage and transport must be safe, suitable and without risk to health.

Manufacturers, suppliers, installers and anyone responsible for maintenance and handling a defective product is liable to you and anyone employed by you or injured on your premises. The employer, however, still has primary responsibility even if an accident is due to someone else's careless or intentional act.

Designers, manufacturers, importers and suppliers of goods are responsible for them, unless the buyer carries out his or her own safety checks. But, unless you can reasonably rely on someone else's research, you must give proper instructions for use and carry out research to minimise health and safety hazards.

Claims for compensation for personal injury must usually be made within three years of the injury and may be reduced to reflect a claimant's own carelessness. The employer must carry compulsory insurance and a copy of the policy must be displayed on your premises unless you only employ close relatives or independent contractors. Employees can also claim for industrial injury under the Social Security Act 1975, payable by the Department for Work, Family and Pensions.

Employees' responsibilities

Employees must follow reasonable orders and safety regulations and take reasonable care of themselves and anyone else affected by their work. The law assumes they work carefully, competently and reasonably skilfully and take proper care of your property, but if there is an accident you may be liable for employing unsuitable people. Even if you specifically forbid an action, you are usually responsible for damage caused by an employee in the course of his or her employment, although the employee may be wholly or partly liable for his or her own deliberate and voluntary act which puts him- or herself and others at risk.

Employer's vicarious liability

You and your business can be convicted for offences committed by an employee which are regarded as your offences – for instance, if your lorry is on the road with an insecure load – and for an employee's negligence or theft on the job. Offences must be seen in the context of the harm they are designed to avoid and there are some defences but, broadly, the test is would a reasonable man say:

■ that the employee's act is part and parcel of the employment, even though unauthorised or prohibited – *vicarious liability and employer liable*; or

■ that it is so divergent as to be plainly alien to it – *employee liable*?

In transactions with businesses – but not consumers – you can exclude civil liability by contract. But it must be reasonable for the risk to fall on the other party and the clause must be clear, unambiguous and brought to the other party's attention before you contract.

Independent contractors and the self-employed

Independent contractors and the self-employed have their own responsibilities. They must not expose co-workers to risk but even if contracts provide for split liability, all the responsibility falls on one party if the other is unable to pay compensation.

Temporary workers

Responsibility for and to temporary workers depends on whether they have a contract of employment or have worked sufficiently long for you to be considered their employer. If engaged through an agency, you are responsible for them only if there is a personal obligation to do the work or the agency is a placement bureau.

Factories

When employees do manual work for pay the premises are transformed into a factory and brought within the ambit of the Factories Act and the employer in 'control' of the premises takes on occupier's liability. Even running a self-service car wash may give sufficient control, although a 'responsible employee' may also wholly or partly share liability.

The Act aims to protect workers in an industrial environment against risks to which they are exposed daily. There must therefore be a safe system of work, the premises and access must, so far as is reasonably practicable, be made and kept safe and potentially dangerous machinery must be fenced. Floors, steps, stairs, passages and gangways must be soundly constructed and maintained and, so far as is reasonably practicable, be free from obstruction and substances likely to cause anyone to slip. Liability here may be shared with independent contractors and you should specifically so provide in your contracts with them.

Health and welfare provisions, similar to those applying to offices and shops, are summarised below and the Health and Safety Executive must be given details about the employer, the business, the work and whether any mechanical power is used. Written notification of accidents causing death, or disablement lasting more than three days which precludes normal work, and of certain specified industrial diseases must also be given.

Offices and shops

Under the Offices, Shops and Railway Premises Act 1963:

- An office is any building solely or principally used as an office or for office purposes and to further such activities, including rooms used as staff canteens and storage.
- A shop is premises used for retail trade; and a shop assistant is anyone wholly or mainly engaged to serve customers, take orders or dispatch goods.
- Trade includes buying, selling, retail sale at auction, lending books for profit, hairdressing, barber shops, the sale of refreshments and intoxicating drinks, buildings where wholesalers keep or dispose of stock or to which the public have access to effect their own repairs, premises used to store and sell fuel and staff canteens.

The prospective occupier must give the local authority two copies of a written notice stating his or her intention to take over premises at least a month prior to occupation or use and must notify the local authority of accidents and industrial diseases in accordance with the 1974 Act.

Health and welfare provisions

Again, the aim is to protect workers in their everyday working environment. The temperature must be comfortable – at least 16°C, or 13°C if severe physical effort is involved. Premises must be clean and sanitary, dirt and refuse must be removed daily, and there are detailed provisions for washing walls and ceilings and redecorating. Drainage must be provided where necessary.

Factories must not be overcrowded and similar provisions apply to the parts of shops and offices which are not open to the public or used for the sale of goods to customers.

Proper and suitable lighting, heating and ventilation must be provided, with sufficient, suitable, clean and properly lit sanitary conveniences. You must provide appropriate and secure changing rooms and comfortable facilities for rest and to eat meals. Drinking water must be accessible. First aid supplies must be kept on the premises with a responsible person in charge – a nurse or person qualified in first aid if there are more than 50 employees. Medical supervision may be required if there is a risk of injury to health, new processes or substances are introduced, or young people are employed.

Employees working with computers on your premises and at their home have special protection and you should:

- Check the workstation and assess and reduce risks.
- Ensure the workstations meet safety requirements.
- Arrange for breaks or changes in the work.
- If appropriate, arrange an eye test.
- Provide health and safety training and information.

Detailed information is available on the Health and Safety website hse. gov.uk and on their infoline: 0845 3450055. The publications orderline is 01787 881165.

Employer protection

Employers can protect themselves by preparing a safety at work scheme after consultation with employees or their trade union representatives, which should be reviewed annually. Protective clothing and equipment with instructions for use should be provided and employees should be reminded of risks. Emergency and safety procedures and directions for the use of protective clothing and equipment should be displayed on the premises. If use of safety equipment is part of the contract of employment or a provision of works' rules, employees can be fairly dismissed – after due warnings – if they do not observe procedures. You should also have the back-up protection of voluntary and compulsory insurance.

Special legislation for certain trades

Some trades require special licences, and you should therefore check with your local authority as to current requirements.

Premises selling food and/or drink, including off-licences, private members' and social clubs, cinemas and anyone organising occasional entertainments must apply to the local council's Licensing Committee for a premises licence. If alcohol is on sale, the person managing the premises must have a personal liquor licence. Public performance by even one musician, professional or amateur, amplified or not, including performances in church or a private club, must also be licensed. There are some exemptions, including broadcasts, purely background music and unamplified music accompanying folk dancing.

A single application covers licences to sell and supply alcohol and to provide regulated entertainment and late-night refreshment. The permission is set out in a single authorisation, either a 'premises licence', a 'club premises certificate' for qualifying clubs or a 'temporary event notice'.

The local authority can serve abatement notices and impose fixed penalty fines or prosecute owners of licensed premises who ignore warnings to reduce noise levels.

The Gaming Act 2005 is to come into force in September 2007. The legislation applies to England and Wales and in part to Scotland; some provisions apply to Northern Ireland.

The local licensing authority – the unitary, district or county council in England and Wales and the licensing board in Scotland – will be responsible for issuing:

- licences for casinos, betting offices, race tracks, bingo clubs and adult gaming centres – the person running the premises requires a personal licence;
- permits for members' clubs, licensed premises and family entertainment centres if gambling is to take place or there are gaming machines on the premises;
- Temporary Use Notices and Provisional Statements for occasional events, involving gambling.

Applications can be made in January 2007 but at the time of writing licence fees had not been fixed.

The Gambling Commission can impose conditions and issue codes of practice but the licensing authority monitors and enforces the legislation and deals with fines and penalties.

Casinos licensed under earlier legislation are unaffected, as their licences will be transferred to the new regime. The licensing authority will continue to register small society lotteries.

Retail shops

You should check with the local authority to find out if there are restrictions on opening hours and if you need permission to load and unload goods before 9.00 am on Sundays.

'Small shops' with a floor area of less than 280 square metres (3,000 square feet) can stay open as long as they like on Sundays, Easter Sunday and Christmas Day but staff may have special employment rights (see page 116).

Shops in England and Wales with a larger floor area may face more restrictions. Many can only open for a continuous period of six hours between 10 am and 6 pm and cannot open on Easter and Christmas Day. Conspicuous notices of opening hours must be placed inside and outside the shop.

However, Sunday trading rules do not apply to:

- shops selling only or mainly alcohol;
- shops in airports, railway stations and service stations;
- registered pharmacies only selling medicinal products and medical and surgical appliances;
- farm shops mainly selling their own produce;
- shops that wholly or mainly sell motor or bicycle supplies and accessories;
- shops that only supply goods to aircraft or sea-going vessels on arrival at, or departure from, a port, harbour or airport;
- exhibition stands selling goods.

There are substantial fines for failing to comply with the Sunday trading requirements.

Statutory references

Arbitration Act 1996
Christmas Day (Trading) Act 2004
Clean Air Act 1993
Clean Neighbourhoods and Environment Act 2005

Congenital Disabilities Act 1975
Consumer Protection Act 1987
Control of Pollution Act 1974
Disability Discrimination Acts 1995 and 2005
Employers' Liability (Compulsory Insurance) Act 1969
Employers' Liability (Defective Equipment) Act 1969
Environmental Protection Act 1990
Estate Agency Act 1979
Factories Act 1961
Fatal Accidents Act 1976
Gambling (Amendment) Act 1990
Gambling Act 2005
Health and Safety at Work Act 1974
Land Registration Act 2002
Landlord and Tenant Act 1954 (Part II)
Landlord and Tenant Act 1927 and 1988
Landlord and Tenant (Covenants) Act 1995
Latent Damage Act 1986
Law Reform (Contributory Negligence) Act 1945
Law Reform (Miscellaneous Provisions) Act 1934
Licensing Act 2003
Limitation Act 1980
Noise Act 1996
Occupiers' Liability Acts 1957 and 1974
Offices, Shops and Railway Premises Act 1963
Race Relations Act 1976
Rent Act 1977
Sex Discrimination Act 1975
Social Security Act 1975
Sunday Trading Act 1994
Town and Country Planning Act 1971
Unfair Contract Terms Act 1977

6

Tax

A short guide to tax is included for completeness, but your first and best adviser is your accountant, who has a broad general knowledge and experience of finance and the law. Accountants are, however, general practitioners and you are advised to ask to be referred to a specialist for difficult questions of law.

The tax bill

Tax is paid on business profits, but the calculation and amount depends on whether you are personally assessed for tax – as sole trader, partner or director – or whether the business is taxed separately. Sole traders and partners pay tax on business profits, but the company pays its own tax.

The tax on business profits for sole traders and partners is paid in three instalments:

1. 'Interim payments' – payments on account on 31 January.
2. A payment on 31 July in the year of assessment; these are usually 50 per cent of the preceding year of assessment's income tax liability, less tax deducted at source.
3. A payment on 31 January following the end of the year of assessment. This comprises the balance of income tax due plus capital gains tax.

No interim payments are due in the year in which you start business, and if you stop trading or profits fall and you think you are liable to less or no tax, you can make an appropriate claim to Her Majesty's Revenue & Customs (HMRC).

Directors are taxed on their income – that is, salary and dividends. The company pays corporation tax (CT) on profits no later than nine months and one day after the end of the accounting period – that is, on profits for the period for which the company's accounts are drawn up. If you have a close company (see page 7), CT and income tax may also be due on loans to participators and their associates in a close company.

Independent taxation

Married couples are taxed as separate individuals. Income and capital gains are taxed separately. For 2006/07 everyone has a single person's allowance of £5,035, increasing to £7,280 for taxpayers between 65 and 74, and £7,420 for taxpayers over 75. A married couple living together are entitled to married couple's allowance against their tax bill of £2,350 and £6,065 if either was born before 6 April 1935. This increases to £6,135 if either is aged 75 or over; but these higher allowances are scaled back when income exceeds £20,100. The married couple's allowances can be transferred to the spouse paying the higher rate of tax. There is also a blind person's allowance of £1,660.

Child tax credit and working tax credit have replaced working families' and disabled person's tax credits. Rates vary but people on middle incomes may qualify if they pay for childcare. Details can be found on the HMRC website.

Married couples holding joint income-producing assets each bears half the tax on income unless they make a declaration stating assets are not owned equally. Both can claim Enterprise Investment, Venture Capital Trust and Corporate Venturing Scheme reliefs and their own deductions for trading losses, pension contributions and so on. Chargeable gains are also taxed separately.

imagine

Starting or growing a business can be a daunting prospect

Menzies Enterprise can take your business from where it is now to where you want it to be.

If you need your accountants to do more than just accountancy, our experienced team are on hand to deliver informed and proactive advice every step of the way.

To find out more, please contact Paul Hickson, Head of Enterprise

020 8974 7500
phickson@menzies.co.uk

www.menzies.co.uk

menzies | enterprise

giving you a helping hand

Enterprise Investment Scheme

Since its introduction, Menzies has used EIS for many clients over the years. The scheme is used as a method for enticing investors to buy shares by the availability of 20% up front tax repayment.

The investor is also attracted by a tax-free exit so long as the shares are kept for sufficient time (this is now 5 years). Also the investor can benefit from inheritance tax advantages including a possible 100% exemption under the business property relief provisions.

There are plenty of qualifying conditions for a company and Menzies is well placed to assist clients through the process.

To succeed, a company must be carrying on qualifying trade which generally excludes land biased trades (property or farming) and financial services.

No investor may hold more than 30% of the shares in the company and it cannot be controlled by another company. There is also a provision to stop EIS being available where there is a prior connection with the company.

The scheme is only available to companies up to the specified size criteria and only for unquoted companies. The alternative investment market (AIM) is deemed to be unquoted which has meant that some stockbrokers offer EIS/AIM portfolios.

So despite the complexities this is a flexible and tax beneficial tax saving scheme.

Tax Allowable Expenses

One of the most commonly asked questions of a tax advisor is "Can I claim tax relief on this cost?" Fortunately in the majority of cases for genuine business expenses the answer is 'yes'. The principle is that if a cost is incurred wholly and exclusively for the purposes of a business then it will be allowable. There are a few specific areas where the law overrides this general rule.

Common areas of concern are:

Capital or revenue costs

There is a blurred line between what one person might view as an asset for longer term capital and what another might consider a consumable (or revenue) cost. For example, a drill or a saw purchased by a company's maintenance staff could be kept and used over many years whilst the same tools bought by a builder may only last a few months of heavy use before they need to be replaced. The former is a capital cost and thus not immediately deductible against year one profits.

Plant and machinery are given tax relief over their life by the provision of capital allowances.

Timing

There have been a number of tax cases in this area, as the time a payment is made may not be the point at which tax relief is granted. If there is a firm commitment prior to the end of the business's accounting period to make some expenditure, then in most cases the costs will be tax deductible.

A few examples:

- The commitment to repair a business facility is a common example of this kind of cost;
- Unless they are paid within 9 months of the year end and decided upon during the accounting period, staff bonuses are not tax deductible;
- Pension contributions must be paid in an accounting period to obtain tax relief (this is a company or employer contribution);
- The costs of arranging loan finance (arrangement fees etc) are usually paid up front but would be spread over the term of the loan;
- A slow paying debt is not necessarily a bad one for tax purposes.

Disallowable costs

There are a few costs that never get tax relief. The most common of these is entertaining costs, which (apart from some staff entertaining) is never tax deductible.

Mixed-use costs

This is more common in non-corporate situations but can arise for companies. The owner of a business might incur costs which could be partly business and partly of personal benefit. Outside a company the tax charge is simply adjusted for these costs, but within a company this can give rise to many questions from the tax authorities about the costs and often there is the suggestion that they are a possible salary to the beneficiary. Expert advice is essential in this kind of scenario.

National Insurance Contributions

This is a very broad topic and one that is certainly the focus of attention for tax authorities and tax advisors. This focus has gradually increased over the past 20 years as the contributions have been increased.

We have heard of situations where businesses have consultants working for them who are "sorting out their own tax". For the consultant there is the attraction of being master of their own tax destiny along with the perception that less tax will be paid overall.

In general, the self-employed pay less NIC than employees but the benefits they receive longer term are also less. The self-employed would generally get a lower state pension and would have to wait longer before they could draw unemployment benefits.

So can we simply choose to be self-employed? Sadly no.

Each employer must consider the status of the people working for them and bear in mind the tasks etc that are performed. If, for example however the tasks or role could be performed equally by a consultant or an employee there may not be scope to defend the status of a self-employed person in the position. Hence tax and NIC would be required as an employee.

The NIC paid for an employee is not only the amount deducted from the employee's salary but also an employer contribution of 12.8% for all earnings over £97 per week. So there is a big incentive not to employ people from a cost saving perspective.

As stated there is little or no real choice. If the person is genuinely carrying out a task as a consultant and meets the various tests set out in the rules, then their status would be able to be defended. This is an area that is getting increasing attention from the tax authorities as they perceive there are too many people working for businesses on a self-employed basis when they should be employees.

If the tax office can convert someone from consultant into an employee then the tax take is commonly very high, so the cost of non-compliance or not reviewing the position could be large.

Proceed with caution.

For further information or for details on how Menzies could help guide you through these complexities, please contact partner **Simon Massey** at **smassey@menzies.co.uk**

Self-assessment

Sole traders, partners and companies now calculate their own tax bill or ask HMRC to do it for them.

Self-assessment brings heavy responsibilities for the taxpayer. There is an automatic penalty of at least £100 if returns are filed late or rejected. Interest and a surcharge is charged on tax paid late. HMRC pays interest at the same rate on overpayment, which is treated as business income and is therefore taxable.

There are fines of up to £3,000 if you cannot produce evidence to support your calculations. All documents relevant to tax affairs should therefore be retained, such as incidental receipts and details of taxable benefits, including tips and expenses. Traders should retain copies of sale and purchase invoices and a daily record of goods taken from stock for private use and goods and services bartered with other traders. If telephones and cars are for both private and business use, itemised bills should be appropriately marked to show which charges relate to the business. The self-employed and companies should retain these records for six years from 31 January following the tax year and employees for about two years, or from the end of the accounting period, and employers for three years. HMRC can take proceedings up to 21 years after the end of a company's accounting period if there is negligence or fraud and can charge a tax-related penalty of up to a maximum of the understated tax.

Tax and the European Union

Basic elements for the harmonisation of *corporate* tax systems have been agreed, but are not yet implemented.

The uniform business rate (UBR)

This is a local property tax paid by occupiers of business premises based on rateable value (RV), which is determined by market rents and updated (revalued) every five years. The most recent revaluation came into effect on 1 April 2005. The rating list can be inspected at your local authority offices, the local Valuation Office or at www.voa.gov.uk.

If you use part of your home for business, you may be liable for business rates on that part. The extent of business use must, however, be clearly identifiable — for instance, business use of a specific room or a garage.

The local council works out the bill by multiplying the RV by the multiplier or UBR, set by the government every 1 April. The UBR is linked to inflation and expressed as pence in the pound. From 1 April 2005 the higher standard multiplier is 43.3p and the multiplier applying to businesses eligible for Small Business Rate Relief is 42.6p. With an RV of £10,000, the bill is £4,260, before applying any transitional or other reliefs. Full details can be found on www.local.dtlr.gov.uk/financial/busrats/guide.

A free leaflet, 'Business Rates Advice', is obtainable from the Royal Institute of Chartered Surveyors. Your local Valuation Office can advise you on how to appeal if you think you are paying too much.

The sole trader and the partnership

The sole trader and the partners are personally liable for tax on business profits, and retiring partners take their tax liability with them. If they die, it passes to their estates.

If you are self-employed you must register with the Revenue within three months of starting work or you may have to pay a fine of £100. Details are available on 08459 15 45 15; if you do construction work you may have to register with the Construction Industry Scheme and obtain a Subcontractors Tax Certificate or Registration Card. Details are available at your local Inland Revenue Office or on the Subcontractors' helpline, 0845 300 0581.

Although the partners are separately assessed to income tax, the partnership must send in a Partnership (Tax) Return setting out the partnership's profits or losses and showing how they are divided between the partners.

If annual turnover is less than £15,000, you do not have to provide detailed accounts and information in your tax return, but can instead submit a simple three-line summary.

The sole trader is taxed as if business income is his or her income. Both sole traders and partners are personally liable for tax deducted from employees' pay and partners are personally liable for tax on their share of partnership income, which must be included in their tax return.

For your first year, you pay tax on a current-year basis on profits from your start date to the following April. The second period is generally 12 months ending on a date that is then your usual 'year end' or 'accounting' date.

Some business expenses, such as wages, rent and rates, qualify for tax relief if incurred not more than three years before you start trading.

For 2006/07, sole traders and partners – like employees – pay tax on income less personal tax reliefs at 10 per cent (the starting rate) on the first £2,150, at 20 per cent (the basic rate) on earnings between £2,151 and £33,300 and 22 per cent on earned income excluding dividends. The higher rate of 40 per cent is payable on income over £33,300.

If you hold shares in a company, you pay an additional 10 per cent income tax on dividends of between £31,150 and £33,300 and 32.5 per cent on dividend income exceeding £33,300.

Unlike employees, sole traders and partnerships can deduct from profits day-to-day (revenue) expenses wholly and exclusively incurred in carrying on business. The previous year's losses are also deductible against income. Any balance remaining can be carried forward and set off against future profits or carried back and set off against earlier profits. Losses in the first four years' trading can be set off against earlier income from any other source in the three years before starting the new business, and a limited partner is entitled to tax relief for the full amount of his or her share of the loss, even if it exceeds the original contribution.

Allowable business expenses

The main expenses that can be deducted from profits as revenue expenses are:

- Running costs, including heating, lighting, rent rates, telephone, postage, advertising, special clothing, cleaning and repairs, but *not* improvements (a capital expense). If you live on your business premises, you can claim a proportion, but may then be liable to CGT and business rates.

- Research and development (R&D) costs. As from 12 April 2000 you can claim R&D tax credits if you invest at least £25,000 in the tax year. This allows deduction of 150 per cent (instead of 100 per cent) of qualifying expenditure, plus a cash payment of £24 for every £100 if the company is not making profits. Staff wages and relevant consumables constitute qualifying expenditure, as well as some costs of subcontracting R&D.
- Goods bought for resale and materials for manufacturing, but *not* plant, cars or machinery (capital expenses), although some smaller items may be allowable.
- Carriage, packing and delivery costs.
- Wages, including your spouse's and the directors, but *not* a sole traders or the partners'.
- Interest on business loans and overdrafts, but *not* on partners' advances.
- Charges for hire, hire purchase and leasing, but *not* the cost price (a capital expense).
- Insurance, but *not* NICs or your life insurance.
- Premiums for employees' liability insurance, including directors' and officers' liability and professional indemnity insurance, and payment of work-related uninsured liabilities.
- Subscriptions to professional and trade organisations.
- Expenses of business trips, but *not* travel between home and a fixed place of work.
- Car running expenses, plus the cost of fuel used for business purposes. Up to £5 (£10 when abroad) for employees' personal expenses when away from home on business.
- Other overseas expenses – weekend and overnight conferences – may also be deductible.
- The cost of an annual staff party to a maximum of £150 per head per annum.
- Some professional fees, eg audit fees, legal advice and the cost of legal proceedings relating to the business, but *not* penalties for breaking the law, eg fines.

- Bad debts, but *not* a general provision for a percentage of unspecified bad debts.
- VAT on business expenses, eg petrol, but *not* if you are a taxable trader for VAT purposes.
- Charitable gifts, including gifts of shares to charities.
- Long service awards after at least 20 years' service of £50 for each year of service.
- Business gifts, but not cash of up to £50 per annum to any one recipient.
- Donations to Learning and Skills Councils.

Companies' allowable expenses against profits are similar to those for the sole trader and partnership, except you can also deduct directors' pay. If there is no dispute, the company can claim repayment of income tax (eg deducted at source on interest received) and tax credits (on UK dividends) before profits are agreed.

Homeworkers

Payments of up to £2 a week to employees working at home are not taxable. Anything over £2 is taxable, unless there is evidence of additional household costs.

Capital allowances

For both income tax and CT, the depreciation to be deducted in the accounts is replaced by capital allowances, which are deducted from the tax bill. The main capital allowances are:

- *Private cars:* 100 per cent first year allowance (FYA) for:
  - new cars for business use with CO_2 emissions of a maximum of 120 grams per kilometre;
  - gas and hydrogen refuelling equipment at refuelling stations *provided* the car is unused, not secondhand and first registered on or after 17 April 2002, or is an electric car and purchased between 17 April 2002 and 31 March 2008;

- cars costing over £12,000 – annual allowance of not more than £3,000;
- Allowances for leased or hired cars are restricted unless they have low CO_2 emissions if the contract is concluded and the hire period begins 1 April 2008;
- CO_2 emission figures are on the vehicle registration document or obtainable from the Vehicle Certification Agency's website www.vc.go.uk.

■ *Plant and machinery:* Natural gas and hydrogen refuelling equipment purchased between 17 April 2002 and 31 March 2008, 'green' technology assets for leasing, letting or hire and energy-saving and water efficient plant and machinery: 100 per cent FYA, thereafter 25 per cent pa on the reducing balance *or* 6 per cent pa for long-life assets, ie plant and machinery with a useful economic life of more than 25 years

but

small businesses paying CT tax can claim 50 per cent FYAs for most plant and machinery purchased on or after 1 April 2004–6 April 2004 if the business pays income tax plus 100 per cent FYA on expenditure incurred between 1 April 2000 and 31 March 2004 on information and communications technologies.

Companies must disclaim allowances if they do not wish to use them, but claims can be amended at a later stage.

Research and development (R&D)

R&D allowances (RDAs) apply to capital expendure, ie purchases of equipment *not* land and dwellings. RDAs are normally 100 per cent of qualifying expenditure but if a disposal for value is brought into account for the expenditure in the chargeable period, the RDA is 100 per cent of the expenditure less the disposal value.

You do not have to claim the full 100 per cent but you cannot claim the balance at a later stage. There is no balancing allowance. There is a balancing charge if there is a later disposal event which exceeds the amount of unclaimed RDA. The balancing charge is the lesser of the amount by which the disposal value exceeds unclaimed RDA, and the RDA.

R&D tax relief – the small and medium-sized companies (SME) scheme

This allows a deduction for SMEs, not sole traders or partnerships, of 150 per cent of qualifying expenditure on R&D in calculating taxable profit. The company must have fewer than 250 employees and annual turnover of under £34.3 million or a balance sheet total under £29.5 million.

Qualifying conditions include:

■ There must be annual R&D qualifying expenditure of at least £10,000.
■ The company must be entitled to ownership of any intellectual property.
■ This must be the only notified state aid for the project.
■ No credit can be claimed for expenditure funded by someone else.
■ There must be no contract to carry out the activities.

But if the last three conditions are not met you may be able to claim under the large company scheme. This requires the work to be relevant to your trade and to be revenue expenditure incurred on either:

■ consumable items;
■ consumable stores;
■ software;
■ staffing;
■ external provided workers.

Or it requires the work to be relevant to your trade and to be revenue expenditure on work contracted by your company to be carried out by:

■ a qualifying body;
■ an individual;
■ a partnership, each member of which is an individual.

Details of both schemes can be found on HMRC's website.

Rollover relief

This relief allows tax arising on the sale of business assets to be deferred or 'rolled over' if the proceeds are used to acquire another qualifying business asset.

Claims can be made up to five years from the 31 January in the year following the tax year when: the old asset is disposed of, or – if later – the new asset is acquired.

The deferred charge is reinstated when the replacement asset is sold.

Stock relief

Stock must be valued at each accounting date. To take account of inflation, HMRC allows a relief calculated by applying the increase in value (based on the 'All Stocks Index' to March 1984) to the value at the beginning of the period. Special provisions apply to the first period of trading and you can make a partial claim or apply for succession relief.

Benefits in kind

Directors and employees whose annual salary is £8,500 and over (including benefits) have to pay tax on their income, plus the cash equivalent of the benefit.

Exemptions for computers and mobile phones loaned to employees

Employees loaned a computer for private use are liable to tax. They are not liable for tax on the loan of one mobile phone but will be charged to tax if they borrow a second phone.

Company car taxation

You pay tax on private use of a company car, including journeys to and from work. For 2006/07 the tax payable is calculated by multiplying the price of the car (usually the list price plus accessories, less capital contributions) by the 'appropriate percentage' based on the car's approved CO_2 emissions figure, with some supplements and reductions to take account of the different fuels set out in Table 6.1.

Table 6.1   Tax on private use of company cars

Fuel type	Code	Standard adjustment	Other Adjustments
Petrol	P	none	none
Diesel (not Euro IV)	D	Supplement 3%*	none
Diesel Euro IV first registered on or before 31 Dec 05	L	Cancel type D supplement above	none
Diesel (Euro IV) first registered on or after 1 Jan 06	L	Supplement 3% (as Type D)*	none
Electric only	E	Reduction 6%	none
Hybrid electric	H	Reduction 3%	none
Gas only	B	Reduction 2%	none
Bi-fuel with CO_2 emissions figure for gas	B	Reduction 2%	use lowest CO_2 figure
Bi-fuel conversion, other Bi-fuel conversion or other			
Fuel not within type B	C	none	none

*subject to overall maximum appropriate percentage of 35%.
Cars approved as bi-fuel cars first registered on or after 1 January 2000 have two approved CO_2 emission figures, one for petrol and one for gas, although only one may be on the Vehicle Registration Certificate.
Supplements and reductions apply only to cars first registered on or after 1 January 1998, whether or not they have an approved CO_2 emissions figure.

Van benefit

Employees pay the following amount of tax for the use of vans available for private use, including journeys to and from work.

Table 6.2 Rates for employees using vans for private use, including journeys to and from work

Type	Years 2007/08	Years from 2007/08
Van less than 4 years old at the end of the tax year	£500	£3,000
All other vans	£350	£3,000

Fuel-only mileage rates

Employees using their own cars for business can claim the fuel allowances in Table 6.3 based on HMRC's Advisory Fuel Rates for Company Cars from 1 January 2006.

Table 6.3 Rates for tax and NIC free mileage allowances for employees using their own vehicle

	Rate per mile
Cars up to 10,000 business miles	40p
Cars over 10,000 business miles	25p
Motor cycles	24p
Bicycles	20p

NB The amounts are accepted for VAT purposes if employers retain receipts
Additional passenger rate: 5p per mile free of tax for each paying passenger travelling on a business journey.

VAT scale charge: VAT due per quarter per car

VAT scale charges are as shown in Table 6.4.

Table 6.4 VAT scale charges per month for fuel

	Scale charge	Petrol	Scale charge	Diesel
Up to 1400 cc	260	£38.72	86	£12.81
1401–2000 cc	346	£51.53	86	£12.81
Over 2000 cc	508	£75.66	110	£16.38

Congestion charges

The London congestion charge is part of your business travelling expense and is deductible for tax purposes if it is wholly and exclusively incurred for the purpose of business. Employees can be reimbursed without incurring any liability to tax if you obtain a 'dispensation' from your PAYE tax office. Other cities are considering imposing a similar charge.

The Enterprise Investment Scheme (EIS)

The EIS is a form of high risk, high return sponsorship where an outsider invests between £500 and an annual maximum of £400,000 in unquoted company shares to fund a start-up business and retains the shares for three years. The various IT and CGT reliefs include:

- income tax relief on up to half the amount invested in the first six months of the year to a maximum of £50,000 can be carried back to the previous tax year *but* dividends are taxable and the relief is clawed back if the shares are sold within three years;
- relief for any allowable losses against income OR chargeable gains;

- loss on disposal of shares is an allowable loss for CGT purposes;
- deferral of CGT on disposal if the gain is reinvested in shares.

No inheritance tax is payable if the shares are held for two years. The scheme covers most businesses but some are excluded, including financial services and overseas companies.

The Venture Capital Trust (VCT) Scheme

VCTs are companies listed on the Stock Exchange that invest in small higher risk unquoted trading companies. The Scheme covers the same businesses as the EIS and the investor can spread the risk over several qualifying companies obtaining:

- income tax relief at 30 per cent on an investment in new ordinary shares with an annual limit of £200,000 – the shares must be retained for at least five years;
- deferral of CGT on disposal if the gain is invested in shares for which IT relief is obtained;
- exemption from CGT on disposal of ordinary shares;
- exemption from IT on ordinary share dividends.

Corporate Venturing Scheme (CVS)

This is another tax incentive scheme to encourage companies to invest in small higher risk unquoted trading companies enabling the investor company to:

- obtain corporation tax relief at 20 per cent on amounts invested in new ordinary shares held for at least three years;
- defer tax on gains which are reinvested in another shareholding under the scheme;
- claim relief against income for capital losses net of corporation tax relief on disposals of shares.

Some small companies whose income mainly derives from licence fees and royalties are included in the Scheme. The corporate investor's maximum stake cannot exceed 30 per cent and individual shareholders in the small company must retain at least 20 per cent of the small companies share capital.

Corporation Tax (CT)

The rates of CT for 2006/07 are shown in Table 6.5.

Table 6.5   Corporation tax rates

Starting rate	0%	on	£0–10,000
Small company rate	19%	on	£50,001–300,000
Marginal relief		on	£300,001–1,500,000
Main rate	30%	on	£1,500,000 plus

The marginal relief fraction for profits between £10,000 and £50,000 is 19/400 and for profits between £300,000 and £1,500,000 is 11/400.

Profits are adjusted by the various allowances and deductions to calculate taxable profit for CT are based on the relevant accounting period. Losses can be carried back against the previous year's profits. A three-year carry-back is available for losses arising in the last 12 months before cessation.

A notice to deliver the Company Tax Return is sent to the company between three and seven weeks after the end of its accounting period, requiring the completed Tax Return for a period of not more than 12 months to be sent to the Revenue by the statutory filing date, ie within three months of receipt of the Notice or 12 months after the end of the accounting period, depending on when the Notice is received and the company's accounting date.

The Tax Return is a self-assessment of the company's tax liability and you must send in accounts drawn up in accordance with the Companies Acts or computations showing how the figures have been arrived at from the figures in the accounts, and the other documents required by the Companies Acts, such as the directors' report, the auditors' report and details of close company's loans to participators and their associates.

Profits are adjusted by the various allowances and deductions to calculate taxable profit for CT based on the relevant accounting period.

Accounting records should be retained for at least six years from the end of the accounting period, either originals or an acceptable alternative form, eg in an optical imaging system or other system which shows you have made a complete and correct Company Tax Return and you must retain original vouchers for tax deducted or tax credits.

Payment is made in a lump sum nine months after the end of the accounting period electronically through BACS and CHAPS or by GIRO or cheque to your company's Inland Revenue Accounts Office at Cumbernauld or Shipley. Interest on late payments is a deductible business cost and interest paid by the Revenue on early payments and over-payments is taxed as income.

The Revenue has at least 12 months to question the assessment. The company is notified of an enquiry and when it finishes and of any adjustments in the tax due.

Contact your local Inland Revenue Enquiry Centre if in doubt as to the deadline for payment or what has to be done.

Employees can buy, or acquire options to buy, company shares under various schemes. Savings attract tax-free bonuses, and there are tax advantages for the company and employees when shares are sold at a profit, but before setting up a scheme you should take expert advice.

Inheritance Tax (IHT)

IHT for 2006/07 on lifetime gifts over £285,000 is 20 per cent but no IT is payable on transfers under £285,000 or any transfers by individuals unless made within seven years of death. Tapering relief applies to transfers made between three and seven years of death. Thereafter the rate is 40 per cent. The threshold increases to £300,00 in 2007/08, £312,000 in 2008/09 and £325,000 in 2009/10.

Capital Gains Tax (CGT)

Capital gains for individuals and companies are taxed as income. The amount chargeable to CGT is added to the individual's income and is chargeable at the rate paid on the top slice of income. Companies pay at the CT rate. Disposals for 2006/07 are exempt where the real or notional gain is less than £8,800. CGT up to the starting rate for IHT and CT is charged at 10 per cent, at 20 per cent between the starting rate and basic rate or small company rate limits and thereafter at 40 per cent. Gains up to March 1998 are reduced by increasing allowable expenditure in accordance with the increase in the retail price index.

Disposal of the business is liable to tax but if you sell and buy another business within three years, you can defer payment until you finally dispose of the new business and stop trading. The relief is particularly helpful if you have been using your home as business premises and claiming tax relief for part of the running expenses.

Disposal of business assets

Tapering relief applies to disposals of business assets after 6 April 2000, including shares held by full and part-time employees in unquoted and quoted trading companies, and shares where a holder of not less than 5 per cent of the voting shares is not an employee. See Table 6.6.

Table 6.6   Tapering relief

Period asset held in years after 1998	Percentage of gain chargeable
0–1	100%
1–2	50%
2–10	25%

Value Added Tax (VAT)

As from 1 April 2006 if annual taxable outputs of the business (charges for goods and services) exceed or are likely to exceed £61,000 including VAT, you must register with HM Revenue & Customs (HMRC) for VAT. The limit is based on the past 12 months' turnover and if at the end of a month, taxable supplies in the last 12 months exceed the limit or might do so in the next 30 days, registration is compulsory. You can apply for registration if turnover is below the limit but there is a discretion to refuse it.

If you think your annual turnover will not reach £54,000 excluding VAT, you can apply for cancellation.

You can account for VAT based on actual receipts and payments instead of invoice dates if your annual turnover excluding VAT does not exceed £660,000. You can continue on this basis for six months after annual turnover excluding VAT reaches £825,000.

If you have not registered for VAT and dispose of capital assets and obtain a VAT refund you may have to pay over the VAT to HMRC.

Invoices must show your VAT-registered number and details of sales including the rate charged and the amount and that they be available for inspection. VAT returns must be completed at the end of the VAT accounting period to show total outputs and the VAT charged. Against this is set total inputs and the VAT paid. If outputs exceed inputs, the balance must be paid to HMRC and if you paid out more than you received, you can claim the difference.

Loans, some property transactions, insurance and some types of education and training are exempt from VAT and are not part of taxable turnover. Some services from abroad, such as advertising, data processing, consultancy and legal, accounting and professional services, are treated as if you supplied them and included in your taxable turnover.

There are special schemes for retailers and special rules for discounts, free gifts, samples, hire purchase and 'self-supply'. The 'flat rate scheme' for businesses with annual turnover excluding VAT of less than £150,000 or annual 'total turnover' of under £187,000 permits you to calculate your VAT payment as a flat rate percentage of turnover. 'Total turnover' is the value including VAT of all business supplies, including exempt and non-business income and the percentage is decided according to the type of business. Property conversion, renovation work and installations of energy-saving materials and heating equipment are liable to VAT at 5 per cent instead of the current 17.5 per cent rate. Bad debt relief is available.

Records must be kept for three years and you complete your obligation as your own tax collector when you post the completed form and appropriate payment to the VAT man.

Up-to-date information is available at www.direct.gov.uk, and from the National Advice Service on 0845 010 9000.

PAYE

Employers are responsible for deducting PAYE from wages and paying it over monthly to the Revenue – including PAYE from their own salary. Small employers with a monthly bill for PAYE and NICs of less than £1,500 a month can pay quarterly. Deductions are based on the tax code number and the Revenue supply tables. Employees must receive Form P60 with details of pay and tax deductions at the end of the tax year. Form P35 goes to the Revenue, summarising their tax and NICs. Leaving employees must receive a P45 – part of which goes to your tax office – to hand to their new employer to ensure the tax record continues.

National Insurance Contributions (NICs)

All employees over the age of 16 and under State Pension age (65 for men and 60 for women) and their employers pay NICs. Payments build up entitlement to social security benefits, including the State Pension. Rates for the tax year 2003/04 2006/07 are shown in Table 6.7.

HMRC's website has information about tax, NICs, telephone helplines and Business Support Teams. Their Employer CD ROM contains forms and built-in calculators to help you work out PAYE, tax, NICs, benefits and Statutory Payments.

Table 6.7 National Insurance Contributions for 2006/07

Class 1
Primary contributions (employee) standard rate

Weekly earnings	Not contracted-out rate	Contracted-out rate
Below £97.00	0%	0%
£97.01–£645	11%	9.4%
Over £645	1%	1%

Secondary contributions (employee)

Weekly earnings	Not contracted-out rate	Contracted-out rate (COSR scheme)	Contracted-out rate (COMP scheme)
Below £97.00	0%	0%	0%
£97.01–£645	12.8%	9.3%	11.8%
Over £645	12.8%	12.8%	12.8%

NB
1 COSR = contracted-out salary related.
2 COMP = contracted-out money purchase.
3 The contracted-out rate only applies to earnings between the lower and upper earnings limits.
4 Some women pay contributions at the reduced rate of 4.85% of earnings.
5 Employer contributions on earnings above the upper limit are assessed at the appropriate not contracted-out rate.
6 The employee's rebate (at 1.6%) on earnings between £84 per week, £364 per month and £4,368 pa (the Lower Earnings Limit – LEL) and £97 per week, £420 per monthly and £5,035 pa (the Earnings Threshold – ET) is deductible from the employee's total contributions or in some circumstances from the employer's remittances to HMRC.
(The Upper Earnings Limit – UEL – is £645 per week, £2,795 per month and £33,540 pa).
7 The employer's rebate (at 3.5% and 1% respectively on earnings between the LEL and the ET) is deductible from remittances to HMRC.

The total minimum Class 1 payment to a contracted-out money purchase pension scheme (COMP) is 2.6% of earnings between the lower and upper earnings limits comprising 1.6% from the employee and 1.0% from the employer.

Class 1A
12.8% is payable in respect of benefits and expenses to directors and employees earning over £8,500. Payment is due by 19 July or 21 July if paid electronically. Payment gives no National Insurance benefit rights.

Other classes
Class 2 Self-employed £2.10 per week on earnings over £4,465 pa
Class 3 Voluntary   £7.55 per week
Class 4 Self-employed 8% on profits between £5035 and £35,540 pa, 1% thereafter. If earnings are less than £4,465 you may be entitled to the Small Earnings Exception (SEE).

No NICs are due if state retirement age is reached by the previous 6 April.
NB Employees earning less than the LEL are treated as having paid NICs when claiming benefit, so you must keep their details on Form P11 or equivalent and report to the Revenue at the end of the year on Form P14.

Pensions

The sole trader or partner is entitled to the self-employed person's State flat-rate pension at retirement age which is not related to previous income. Premiums on self-employed policies are not allowable against income.

Employees, including directors, with earnings above a certain level (£4,368 in 2006/07) cannot leave the basic State Pension scheme but they can 'contract out' of the State Second Pension (S2P – formerly SERPS) by joining a private pension scheme. If the business does nothing, it has 'contracted in', 'not contracted out' NICs apply and employees receive the State Pension. If you contract out, you pay lower NICS and make your own pension arrangements.

Tax relief

Tax relief on pension contributions depends on whether you pay into a personal or pension scheme that covers all your employees.

With schemes covering all your employees the employer deducts contributions from the employee's pay before deducting tax and the employee pays tax on the balance. Higher rate taxpayers obtain full tax relief immediately.

With personal pensions the pension provider claims tax back from the government at the basic rate of 22 per cent, so every £78 paid into the pension puts £100 in the pension pot. Higher rate taxpayers can claim the difference through Self Assessment or by letter to their Tax office.

From April 2006 you can put as much as you like into any number of personal and/or company pensions and there is no upper limit on pension savings. You can claim tax relief of up to 100 per cent of earnings to a maximum annual allowance of £215,000 in 2006/07, rising to £255,000 in 2010; the lifetime limit is £1.5m in 2006/07, rising to 1.8m in 2010.

In the light of the April 2006 changes the maximum annual tax-efficient gross contribution to age 75 is:

■ £3,600 or 100 per cent of earnings to £215,000 for an individual;
■ £215,000 less employee contributions for employers.

Only current earnings count for the 100 per cent limit in 2006/07.

This is, however, a complicated area and you should seek expert advice before committing yourself.

Contracted-out pension schemes

Members of Contracted-Out Salary-Related schemes (COSRs), Contracted-Out Money Purchase schemes (COMPs), Contracted-Out

Mixed Benefit schemes (COMBs) and contracted-out occupational pension schemes and their employers pay lower NICs. Employees contracted-out through an Appropriate Personal Pension (APP) pay full rate NICs but the Department for Work and Pensions pays the difference between the contracted-out and non contracted-out rates.

The COSRS pension is based on salary, length of service and annuity rates (the rate at which the pension fund is converted into a pension) on retirement. Employer and employee make contributions and the scheme must comply with certain legal standards.

COMPS provide a flat-rate refund of NICs (the minimum payment) paid in by the employer, plus an age-related top-up (the age-related rebate (ARR)), paid by the Department of Social Security. Employers and employees usually make extra contributions, for which they receive tax relief.

COMBs have separate benefit and money purchase sections, both of which contract out.

Employers and employees contributing to occupational pension schemes pay lower NICs. On retirement employees receive a second pension from the employer's scheme plus S2P if they have paid into it.

Some occupational pension and personal pensions schemes are organised on a 'rebate-only' basis, ie the only money paid in is the employee's NICs. On retirement employees receive about the same amount they would from S2P.

Stakeholder pension schemes are low-cost schemes for employees earning more than the LEL (£77 per week, £334 a month and £4,004 pa), who do not have the right options available to save for retirement. You must arrange access to this sort of scheme unless:

- you employ fewer than five people; or
- you offer all employees over 18 a personal pension scheme through which you contribute an amount equivalent to at least 3 per cent of their basic pay; or
- you offer an occupational pension scheme they can join within a year of starting work.

Arranging access does not mean you must set it up and run the scheme. Commercial financial services can do it, and register the scheme with the

Inland Revenue and Occupational Pensions Regulatory Authority. It is, however, up to the employees whether they wish to join the scheme.

Personal pension premiums paid on or after 6 April 2001 attract immediate basic rate tax relief at source. Premiums paid on 6 April 2002 can be carried back to 2002/03 to use up unused relief from earlier years.

Statutory references

These are kept to a minimum; further details are available from HMRC and the DWP and their websites.

Capital Allowances Acts 1968 and 1990
Companies Act 1985
Employee Share Schemes Act 2002
Finance Acts 1965, 1966, 1972, 1975, 1976, 1980, 1982, 1984 to 2003
Finance Act (No 2) 1997
Income and Corporation Taxes Acts 1970 and 1988
Pensions Act 1995
Pensions Schemes Acts 1993 and 1995
Income and Corporation Taxes Acts 1970 and 1998*l*
Income Tax (Earnings and Pensions) Act 2003
Income Tax (Trading and Other Income) Act 2005
Taxation of Chargeable Gains Act 1992
Tax Credit Act 2002
Social Security Act 1998
Social Security Contributions and Benefits Act 1992 as amended
Value Added Tax Act 1994

7

Insurance

Insurance is a gamble and you can cover almost any risk at a price. The only real difference between insurance and placing a bet is that insurance contracts are enforceable in English law.

The insurance contract

First you submit a proposal – application – to a broker or insurer giving details of the risk. The insurance contract is complete when your offer is unconditionally accepted, although the insurer can accept subject to payment of the premium. Non-marine policies can be agreed verbally if the items, the sum insured and the risks are specified. With other insurance you can, if those terms are agreed, be covered pending formal acceptance but the insurer can withdraw after making enquiries.

Cover can be arranged informally on issue of a cover note. This is a temporary contract, distinct from the formal policy, unless the insurer combines them by sending the cover note on receipt of the premium as a 'deposit receipt'. Temporary cover notes renewing existing policies do not extend cover automatically and may be only an offer to insure, requiring acceptance. The note becomes a deposit receipt when the premium is paid. Some policies are self-extending but if not, a new policy must be agreed, unless cover is renewed on the 'usual' or 'previous' terms.

The law of the contract

If you trade abroad insurance may be governed by foreign law, unless the contract states it is to be governed by English law. Who receives the payment depends on the law of the place where the money is payable – whether money is owed is governed by the law of the contract but who receives it is governed by the law where it is to be paid out. Money is usually payable where insurers carry on business but life policies pay out in accordance with the law where the deceased was domiciled on death.

Terms and conditions

Legally, insurance contracts are contracts of *uberrimae fidei*. That is, they are made in 'the utmost good faith' and the parties must disclose everything affecting the risk. A mistake or inadequate disclosure may amount to misrepresentation and changes to the risk may invalidate the policy.

You can agree values initially under a 'valued policy'. Claims are based on that value but usually cover is limited to a specific amount, which is the maximum you can claim. Overvaluation can lead to cancellation and if no values are agreed you can usually claim the market value or the cost of repair or restoration to the limit of the sum insured, subject to averaging.

Most policies include an *average clause* that restricts claims to current market values, taking account of depreciation, which is usually less than replacement value. You can insure for replacement cost but premiums are higher.

If cover is only for loss of goods or damage to premises, there is no claim for loss of profits, loss of rent or loss of custom unless included in the policy.

Because you acquire new items to replace those depreciated in value by use, a discount on claims for goods lost or destroyed is usually included but you can, if this is possible, require the insurer to pay for repairs instead.

Most policies set out terms and conditions, some describe legal effects and enlarge or restrict rights and obligations. On careful and expert reading you may discover you are entitled to damages if a claim is refused.

Cover

Claims are based on abnormal circumstances. Normal wear and tear and inherent vice – natural behaviour of the item insured – are usually excluded, even under 'all risks' cover (which means loss or damage caused in the circumstances set out in your policy). Most risks can be covered for a price, including terrorist attack, but riot, act of God, civil commotion and war are usually excluded. Accident policies cover accidents caused by carelessness, including the insured's, but deliberate damage is only covered if someone else is responsible.

Only risks occurring during the currency of the policy are covered. Transit risks are usually covered from the beginning to the end of the trip but you should check that loading and unloading, goods in storage, loaded overnight or unattended are covered and all methods of transport are included, in case there is an unforeseen change of route.

The time of loss is the time of the accident, whenever discovered, except in marine insurance, or if arising from an accident outside the period of cover. Causation can therefore be crucial.

Claims are based on one direct, operative cause – the 'proximate' cause – which cannot be an excepted risk or outside the risk period.

Goods in transit

If you use a 'common carrier', that is, public transport, the carrier insures your goods and is liable for their loss or damage, unless due to an act of God or the Queen's enemies or unless there is an agreement to the contrary. There is no contract between you and the carrier, and the amount you can claim is minimal. You can claim the full value if you declare the value on delivery, but the costs of carriage will then be raised accordingly.

Carriage by sea

Contracts for carriage by sea and contracts of affreightment are incorporated into in a bill of lading (see page 106) or a charter party, and you must insure the goods yourself.

If you deal directly with shippers and need to use all the space in a ship, the contract is usually contained in a bill of lading. This is a document signed by the ship owners, or on their behalf, stating that your goods have been shipped on a specified ship or have been received for payment; when signed by or on behalf of the carrier the bill of lading is handed to the skipper. The bill and the goods can be transferred by endorsement and delivery of the bill but it is not a negotiable instrument.

If you hire a ship directly from the ship owner to carry your goods, however, your contract is contained in 'charter party' which can be either:

■ a voyage charter party – covering carriage in a specified ship from a named port to a named port for one or more voyages;
■ a time charter party – covering carriage for a specified period; or
■ a charter party by demise – where you have complete control of the ship, its navigation and your own master and crew.

Marine insurance

Marine insurance covers 'maritime perils' incidental to 'marine adventures', ie ships and goods exposed to maritime perils and lost or damaged goods travelling by sea. You can extend the cover to inland waters.

Marine insurance contracts are made when the proposal is accepted by the insurer. Usually a document is issued – the 'slip' – which is a short memorandum of the contract when it is accepted by the underwriter. The broker acts as your agent and offers the slip to insurers, such as the underwriting syndicates at Lloyd's. Each agent of the syndicate writes a line, ie accepts a limited amount of risk – *pro tanto* – until the full amount on the slip is covered. The slip itself is an offer and the signature of the underwriters, through their agents, is their *pro tanto* acceptance. There is therefore a separate and binding contract between you and each underwriter even before the full amount on the slip is covered, although you cannot sue on the slip until the policy is issued.

You can take out:

■ *voyage policies* – cover from port to port;
■ *time policies* – cover for a specified period;

* *mixed policies* – cover for a specified voyage and period;
* *valued policies* – cover for a specified value;
* *unvalued policies* – where the value is calculated according to a formula and subject to the limit of the sum insured;
* *floating policies* – where details are defined by later declaration.

In marine policies, the value of claims is the value when the goods were insured, not their value at the time of loss and, unless expressly excluded, claims are subject to averaging.

Notice of loss

Notice must be given promptly and in accordance with the policy, with sufficient details to enable the insurer to ascertain the nature of the claim. Verbal notice may be accepted but it is advisable to have a written record.

You may have to prove loss, damage and the amount claimed and must usually report loss or theft to the police or appropriate authorities. Insurers often instruct assessors and loss of profits usually requires assessment by auditors.

Settlement

Claims are usually negotiated and, if substantial or complicated, you should instruct assessors. Entitlement under a cover note or after the renewal date depends on the circumstances and the type of insurance. Most insurers will agree to have liability – not the amount of the claim – decided in court even if there is an arbitration clause, unless you expressly agreed to the clause or it is a marine or aircraft policy.

Acceptance must be unconditional but payment can be recovered if the insurer can prove fraud or a mistake of fact.

Usually settlement is in cash and the insurer is entitled to claim lost or damaged goods as salvage.

Insuring business premises

Insuring the premises

A 1774 statute gives insurers the right to insist on rebuilding or reinstating business premises and, unless the policy sets a limit, they cannot limit the cost and work must be completed within a reasonable time. If damage is caused by fire, a landlord or tenant can force the insurer – but not a Lloyd's underwriter – to rebuild or reinstate unless an occupier is responsible. The insurers do not then have to replace trade or tenants' fixtures and can restrict the cost.

Leasehold premises

Landlord or tenant can insure leasehold premises. The tenant's insurable interest is only as tenant in possession, so he can only recover his own loss, unless liable for the value of the entire premises under a repairing covenant or the general law. Rent usually continues to be payable even if the tenant is not required to repair in the event of fire or the premises are destroyed.

The tenant therefore usually insures at the commencement of the lease if he covenants to repair. The tenant is in breach of covenant if renewal premiums are not paid and the landlord can claim damages or, if there is a right of re-entry for breach of covenant, forfeit the lease.

If the tenant is not bound to insure, the landlord must do so but the tenant is liable for increases in the premium due to changes on his or her own premises and cannot recover under the landlord's insurance although he or she may be entitled to claim reinstatement under the 1774 Act. If the covenant benefits both landlord and tenant, the landlord must reinstate. You can extend fire cover to include 'special perils', including explosions, earthquakes and overflowing of water tanks, apparatus or pipes, on a replacement or reinstatement basis, as well as architects' and surveyors' fees, the building contents, stock, plant, machinery, fixtures and fittings and the removal of debris. Fire insurance can also be restricted, but you are usually covered for your own damage by explosion on your premises but not necessarily for damage to other buildings unless caused by the fire itself.

Types of insurance

Burglary insurance

This covers theft involving forceful or violent entry and the insurer usually requires the premises to be properly protected.

Engineering insurance

Inspection by 'competent' engineers required by the Factories Act is offered by specialist insurers.

Money insurance

Insurance against loss of cash covers loss by any cause except theft by employees (insurable under a fidelity bond or policy – see below) and can include personal assault.

Insuring goods

Claims on goods, other than depreciation, depend on whether they are at your risk and rights may have to be ceded to the insurer. You can insure before you buy under a 'floating policy' covering 'all the goods in the warehouse or otherwise ascertainable' for a fixed amount, a 'declaration policy' for goods to be declared from time to time, or an 'open policy' insuring against all risks by sea and land. There are several commercial variants, including sellers' insurance inclusive CIF (cost, insurance, freight) for the buyer's benefit and FOB (free on board) insurance where the buyer pays premiums. You should check insurance and sales documents to ensure you are adequately covered.

Liability insurance

Liability insurance covers liability to employees and the general public as employer, owner and occupier of a building. Public liability insurance usually covers compensation for injury, disease or damage to the public and can be extended to cover accidents caused by defective goods but not injury to your own employees, damage to your property if you are in occupation and some kinds of liability under commercial contracts.

Because you are usually liable for injuries sustained by employees at work, you must be covered by appropriate insurance with authorised insurers, unless you employ only family or independent contractors. The certificate of insurance must be displayed on the premises and details of injuries kept in an accident book.

Personal accident and/or sickness insurance

Schemes can be set up to provide employees with accident and sickness cover and health insurance.

Motor vehicle insurance

Legally you must carry 'road traffic cover', indemnifying you only against compensation for death or injury to third parties. 'Third-party cover' indemnifies you for damage to third-party property and can be extended to loss and damage to your own vehicle. Comprehensive cover also includes accidental damage to your vehicle.

You must inform the insurer if vehicles are used for business purposes. Even under road traffic cover you are usually insured personally to drive any vehicle but you should check to make sure your policy is automatically transferred if you change your vehicle, it is stolen or destroyed, or if you make a claim.

Fidelity bonds and policies

Employees' theft, breach of confidence and fraud are covered by fidelity bonds and policies. They usually apply to particular employees in a stated capacity for a fixed period and loss arising from default within the period is covered, even if discovered after it. It is not usually necessary to give notice of suspicion.

Credit insurance

Debts are usually insured on the basis of an indemnity (but see pages 169–70 for business done abroad). Cover can be for default on the due date or in specified circumstances. Unless claiming an unpaid balance, you do not usually have to sue the debtor or enforce a security. Your rights are transferred to the insurers on payment but you may have to carry part of the loss. Debts and uncompleted contractual performance can also be covered by guarantees and sureties. Under a guarantee you are guaranteed payment but a surety pays you on default and the principal debt remains unaffected.

Insurance against legal claims

Insurance is available to cover most civil claims brought against you in the courts, including legal costs.

Directors and auditors

Companies can indemnify officers and auditors for liability in some civil or criminal proceedings provided judgment is given in their favour, relief is granted by the court, or they are acquitted. If the Articles permit, additional insurance is obtainable to cover unindemnifiable risk.

Insuring key personnel

You can insure against loss caused by the death of senior management, for instance, to provide cash to buy out a deceased partner's share, or to engage someone to take over management.

Disputes

The Insurance Ombudsman deals with insurance disputes and details are available from the Insurance Ombudsman Bureau's office.

Statutory references

Companies Act 1989
Defective Premises Act 1972
Employers' Liability (Compulsory Insurance) Act 1969
Employers' Liability (Defective Equipment) Act 1969
Factories Act 1961
Fire Prevention (Metropolis) Act 1774
Marine Insurance Act 1906
Occupiers' Liability Act 1957 and 1983
Sale of Goods Act 1979

8

Employers and employees

When you take on employees the law may take an active part in the business. You may have to comply with industrial practice and collective bargaining agreements. The network of legislation is studded with fines and penalties and contravention can prove far more expensive than taking preventive measures.

Employers' obligations

The employment legislation covers all employees, including part-timers, except for:

- close family;
- non-executive directors;
- trainees under youth training schemes;
- employees working abroad;
- the self-employed.

Directors as 'office-holders' are excluded unless they are clearly employees – for instance, there is a service contract.

Self-employed workers are excluded from most of the employment protection and they also have their own responsibilities under health and safety legislation. It is therefore important to know whether your workers are employed by you or by themselves. Key criteria include the job description, when and how payment is made, who pays tax and National Insurance, how far and to what extent the employee is integrated into your business and whether the 'employer' provides equipment and who takes a profit or loss on the work.

Fixed-term employees covers employees:

■ doing 'seasonal' or 'casual' work with contracts ending on a specified date, or when a specified event does or does not happen or a specific task has been completed;

■ on fixed-term contracts specifically covering maternity, parental, adoption or sick leave;

■ hired to cover for peaks in demand where the contract expires when demand decreases;

■ whose contracts expire when a specific task is complete.

They must not be treated less favourably than comparable permanent employees, unless this can be is objectively justified. They are entitled to be told about vacancies and, unless it is objectively justified, to have access to occupational pensions schemes. They may not be entitled to redundancy payments under the terms of their contract *but* failure to renew a fixed-term contract at the end of the term may amount to dismissal and they may be entitled to redundancy payment.

After four years on fixed-term contracts they are considered to have a permanent contract; if offered a further fixed-term contract they are entitled to a written explanation. If this is unsatisfactory, the employer must confirm the contract as open-ended.

Apprentices, students on work experience placements of up to one year for part of a graduate, postgraduate or teacher training course and employees on government-supported training or retraining programmes are not fixed-term employees.

Agency workers

People taken on through employment agencies (which introduce them to the organisation as 'hirers', so that the employer's contract is with the worker, not the agency) or employment businesses (which contract with workers, supplying their services to organisations as 'users') also have statutory protection.

Workers must be vetted, 'temp to perm' fees are restricted, and the agency must state whether it acts as an agency or business and explain the difference. In addition, *employment agencies* must:

■ not contract on behalf of workers or users without authority;
■ give details of charges;
■ give written details to workers of how they will find work.

Employment businesses must:

■ pay workers even if the user does not pay them;
■ not pay or be connected with paying fees to anyone they introduce to a user.

Users must now pay temps themselves or accept supply through an arrangement that may cause problems for businesses that cannot fully recover VAT.

Home workers are entitled to the minimum hourly wage or 120 per cent of the wage for the hours an average worker would take to do the work.

If they use electronic equipment to contact their office base, however, they may be employees or self-employed.

Shift workers doing Sunday and/or night work can be paid:

■ flat-rate allowances, per hour, shift or week, plus basic day rates;
■ fixed percentage additions to day-work rates;
■ basic day work-rates plus a higher rate;
■ standard annual amounts paid to all employees on a specific shift;
■ extra allowances for hours outside normal working hours.

If retirement is not reasonably justified, there may be a claim for unfair dismissal.

Shop workers with the same employer since or before:

- 25 August 1994 in England and Wales;
- 4 December 1997 in Northern Ireland;

and *betting workers* with the same employer since or before:

- 2 January 1995 in England and Wales;
- 26 February 2004 in Northern Ireland;

do not have to work on Sundays and can only agree to do so by giving written, signed and dated opt-in notice.

Workers in Scotland whose contracts require or may require them to work Sundays must work a three-month notice period if they opt out of Sunday work. Employees who are or may be required to work Sundays must receive a written statement explaining their rights within two months of starting work. If not and the employee gives opt-out notice, the three-month notice period is reduced to one month, ie the employee can stop Sunday work after one month instead of the usual three months. The right to opt-in and opt-out is continuous and can be exercised at any time.

Refusal to work on Sundays does not justify dismissal, redundancy or other detrimental treatment, eg refusing promotion. If rights are infringed by the employer there may be a claim for unfair dismissal or detrimental treatment. Procedures are set out on the Department of Trade and Industry website www.dti.gov.uk.

Employee protection

Protection gives rights to guarantee and redundancy payments, minimum periods of notice, compensation for unfair dismissal and other rights listed below. Once agreed, all employees (including part-timers) are entitled to the same sick leave, pensions, holidays, staff discount and share option benefits, including regular part-timers and casual part-time employees working on a day-to-day basis for over three months.

Within two months of starting work, employees must have a *written statement* giving details of employer and employee, a job description, the place of work, the date of starting work and what other work, if any, forms part of the 'continuous period of employment' (increasing the qualifying period for protection under the legislation). Working hours must be set out, the amount and time of payment, disciplinary procedures (but not grievance procedures if there are fewer than 20 employees), details of relevant collective agreements, pension rights, holiday and sick pay, length of notice and details of any contracting-out certificate (relating State pensions to earnings); length of employment must be included for temporary employees. Details of pension schemes, sick pay, disciplinary rules and procedures and notice can instead be in another reasonably accessible document. Employees must receive written notification of changes within a month of the change.

Pay statements must give details of gross and net pay, with details of the amounts and reasons for deductions.

After four weeks' work you and your employees are entitled to a week's notice. After two years employees are entitled to a week's notice for each year of continuous work to a maximum of 12 weeks but they can take payment in lieu.

Hours of work

All employees, including part-time, casual, freelance and agency staff, *but not* managing and executive staff and family members, are entitled to:

- Work no more than 6 days out of 7, or more than 12 out of 14.
- A minimum daily rest period of 11 consecutive hours in 24.
- A rest of 30 minutes every six hours, if working longer than six hours.
- A minimum rest period in seven days of 24 consecutive hours, that is, a full day, plus 11 hours of daily rest. Days off can be averaged over two weeks to give two days off a fortnight.
- A maximum average of 48 hours' work in seven days including overtime.
- A maximum of 48 hours' average working time in seven days.

Employees making their own decisions because of the nature of the job, eg senior managers, can opt out of the working time regulations and the full rest period entitlement does not apply if you agree different working hours.

Employees paid by the hour, paid overtime, working under close supervision or required to work longer hours, eg because of output requirements, cannot opt out but they must not be forced to work more than an average of 48 hours a week.

Young employees – you cannot employ a child under 13, unless he or she comes within the exceptions, eg acting, but working hours are strictly controlled and you usually require a local authority licence.

In England, Wales and Scotland young people between 13 and the minimum school-leaving age of 16 may not do paid or unpaid work:

▆ before 7 am or after 7 pm;
▆ for more than two hours on a school day or Sunday;
▆ for more than 12 hours a week during term time;
▆ for more than 25 hours a week in school holidays OR 35 hours if aged 15 or over.

In Northern Ireland, young people under 15 may not do paid or unpaid work:

▆ for more than two hours on Sunday;
▆ for more than five hours on school days or Saturdays;
▆ for more than 27 hours in any week.

School-age children's work is governed by strict rules even if they only do a paper round. They must not be employed in manufacturing or dangerous activities and you may have to provide evidence the job is not dangerous.

Existing risk assessments must be checked, including health and safety arrangements, taking into account the teenager's immaturity and inexperience. The local authority must be notified and you may need a local authority or local education authority permit.

Employees aged 16 and 17 must:

- work for a maximum of 8 hours a day or 40 hours a week;
- have a break of 30 minutes every four and a half hours;
- have a rest period of 12 hours between each working day;
- have two days off a week.

They can be employed in certain dangerous environments if necessary for training, so long as they are supervised and risks are minimised.

They may be entitled to paid time off for study or training. Employees aged 18 to 24 claiming Jobseeker's Allowance for at least six months may be entitled to two days off a week to study, plus at least one extra day, or its equivalent, for up to six months. Information about financial assistance for employers is available on the Department for Education and Skills (DfES) website www.dfes.gov.uk. Refusing time off for training is a ground for a complaint to the employment tribunal.

Apprentices. Staff aged 16 to 24 may be eligible for apprenticeship and there are proposals to extend the age limit beyond 24. Details of schemes and financial assistance towards the cost of training are available on the Learning and Skills Council website www.lsc.gov.uk and by telephone on 0870 900 6800.

Night workers who work at least three hours between 11 pm and 6 am should only work an average of eight hours, calculated over 17 weeks. They cannot choose to exceed this unless allowed by a collective workforce agreement. They may be able to average night work over a period of 26 weeks *but not* if they deal with special hazards or are under mental and physical strain.

Night workers and employees are entitled to compensatory rest – ie they can accumulate rest periods and defer them to a later date; their average hours are calculated over 26 instead of 17 weeks – if they:

- work a long way from where they live;
- have to travel to different places for work;
- do security or surveillance work;
- have jobs that require round-the-clock staffing;
- work during exceptionally busy periods and emergencies.

'Mobile' employees, working in road, or inland waterways transport, must not work more than:

■ an average of 48 hours per week;
■ 60 hours in any single week;
■ 10 hours in any 24-hour period, if working at night.

They cannot opt out of the average weekly working limit but can extend the reference period from 17 to 26 weeks and the amount of night work by collective or workforce agreement.

You must offer and keep records of free regular health assessments and retain them for two years. You may also need to assess your health and safety implications for night working, eg your fire-evacuation procedures and security arrangements.

Records should be kept to show compliance with working time and night work limits, with details of employees who agree to work more than 48 hours a week. If they seem to be nearing the time limits they should be monitored to ensure compliance with the regulations.

Flexible working hours

Parents, adoptive parents, carers and guardians of children under 6 and disabled children under 18 who have worked for you for at least 26 weeks can apply to you once a year to be permitted to work 'flexible' hours. A refusal must be based on genuine business grounds. You must meet the employee for discussion within 28 days of the application. The employee can bring a companion to the meeting, and 14 days thereafter you must give written notification of agreement and the starting date of the new arrangement, which permanently changes the terms and conditions of employment.

The employee has 14 days to appeal your refusal to ACAS, the employment tribunal or other form of dispute resolution. Refusal must be supported by written reasons. If you lose the appeal, you may be ordered to reconsider, and if the procedure has not been followed you may have to pay compensation of up to two weeks' pay.

Holidays

All workers, other than managing and executive staff and family members, but including those on short-term contracts, are entitled to four weeks' annual paid holiday, which does not include statutory and bank holidays, and to payment in lieu of holidays if the employment ends before they take a break.

Contracts of employment and senior employees' service agreements

The statement is not a contract but is evidence of some terms in a full service contract. This can be oral or written and should include everything in the statement plus a requirement to follow the safety at work scheme, if any, and works' rules put together after consultation with staff or their representatives. (If rules are included, they must be changed by agreement; if not, they can be changed any time.) Changes are accepted if there is no objection within a reasonable time unless the contract permits variation or it can be implied from conduct or a collective agreement. Objection by resignation may be constructive dismissal and also unfair dismissal.

Wages

If payment is not agreed, reasonable remuneration can be claimed for work done.

Employees must be paid not less than the national minimum wage, currently £3.30 per hour for employees aged 16 and 17, and £5.35 for employees aged 18 to 21 and employees during their first six months in a new job with a new employer who receive accredited training. The minimum wage for employees aged 22 and over is currently £5.35.

Apprentices aged 19 to 25 in the first 12 months of their apprenticeship are not entitled to the national minimum wage. If they are funded by the Learning and Skills Council (LSC) in England they receive a minimum income of £80 per week.

If any employees are paid less than the minimum wage, an Enforcement Officer can serve an enforcement notice requiring an employer to pay them the minimum wage for a current and future pay period plus arrears, and if the notice is not complied with the officer or employee can take proceedings in an industrial tribunal to recover underpayments.

Here, 'workers' are employees working under a contract of employment or agreement whereby they undertake to do or perform personally work or services. Clients, customers, the self-employed and members of your family are not workers.

Your records must show payments as an hourly rate, they must be sufficient to show compliance with legislation and must be produced on request to the employee, the enforcement agency, tribunals and courts. HMRC deals with complaints and can enter premises, inspect records and issue enforcement notices. 'Penalty notices' may be served if the notice is not complied with – the employer will be fined and the employee may be awarded additional pay.

Deductions from the wages of 'workers' – here anyone working as an employee or self-employed, including apprentices but not those working directly for customers or clients – are unlawful unless:

■ required or permitted by the law or the contract;
■ the worker has given prior written consent.

And you can lawfully deduct:

■ reimbursement for overpaid wages and expenses;
■ payments made under statutory disciplinary proceedings;
■ statutory payments due to a public authority;
■ amounts due to third parties under contract – eg TU dues – and to satisfy court orders;
■ wages during a strike.

You can also make deductions for cash shortages and stock deficiencies from retail employees' wages to a total of 10 per cent of the gross wage.

Sick pay

You can agree whatever you like about sick pay but employees off sick for at least four consecutive days – including weekends, holidays and days off – can claim Statutory Sick Pay (SSP). SSP is only payable for qualifying days, ie days on which employees are required to work. Nothing is payable for the first three ('waiting') days. Qualifying days during the previous eight weeks when an employee is off sick for at least four consecutive days count towards waiting days and absences of at least four consecutive days link with other absences during an eight-week period. Sickness can be self-certificated on form SC2 but after seven days medical certificates should be provided.

SSP1 must be sent to employees off sick for four or more days who are *not* entitled, or cease to be entitled, to SSP so they can claim Incapacity Benefit.

The daily rate of pay is based on the weekly rate divided by the number of qualifying days in the week for which you pay SSP. Weeks begin on Sunday and each week commencing Sunday that the employee is sick is a separate pay period. SSP is treated like pay, so you must deduct PAYE, tax and NICs. You can also deduct the lawful deductions set out above. When the employee is paid daily or weekly, SSP will be below the NIC lower-earnings limit, but if you make any other payments in the same period – eg wages or occupational sick pay – tax and NICs must be deducted. SSP is included as part of the total year's pay for directors and employees with annual earnings periods.

Records must be kept on HMRC forms, your own computerised forms or magnetic tape and retained for at least three years. Forms and SSP2 records sheets are obtainable free of charge from HMRC, but you can use computerised forms if they include the necessary information.

If employees have more than one job, earnings from each job count separately for NICs and you can share SSP payments with the other employer. If the employee's other job is working for him- or herself, you are liable for the full amount of SSP.

If at least seven days' SSP is due to an employee who leaves the job, you must give a leaver's statement on SSP 1(L) but this is only needed by a new employer if the employee is sick for at least four consecutive days during the first eight weeks.

SSP is currently payable at the rate of £70.05 a week except to employees under 16 and over 65, employees on fixed-term contracts of three months or less and those paid less than £84 per week before deduction of income tax and NICs. Employees receiving statutory paternity or adoption pay cannot also claim SSP.

SSP ceases to be payable after 28 weeks or the employee becomes entitled to Maternity Pay or Allowance. You can recover payments under the Percentage Threshold Scheme (PTS) if total SSP payments exceed Class 1 NICs for the tax month less contracted-out rebate, if any, multiplied by 13 per cent of your NIC liability for the tax month. Records of total gross Class 1 NICs and SSP payments in each month should be entered in your HMRC payslip booklet P30BC, form P32 or your pay records. You can deduct the amount you are entitled to recover from your contributions to HMRC. If you are entitled to recover more than the contributions due, you can deduct the excess from PAYE income tax due that month, entering the excess in the National Insurance box of the payslip, preceded by the letter 'M' (for minus), but *do not* alter the amount entered for PAYE tax.

Even if you have opted out, you can still recover payments up to the amount of SSP due under the PTS and deduct it from payments to the HMRC Accounts Office, but details must be recorded on forms P14 and P35. Write directly to the HMRC Accounts Office at the address on your P30(BC) if you need to recover the payments as a matter of urgency.

Details of the SSP scheme, explanatory booklets and forms are obtainable from HMRC.

You can opt out of the SSP scheme for all or part of your workforce if your occupational sick pay (OSP) scheme offers equivalent or better benefits whether or not your scheme is formalised. You can pay on an informal or discretionary basis, or you can pay the normal wage. You can also choose to pay OSP for a limited period and then opt an employee back into SSP.

You do not have to inform the Revenue if you opt out and you can still claim the amount you could have recovered under the Percentage Threshold Scheme, provided you keep proper records.

This means that you do not have to keep two sets of records (for OSP and SSP) although in practice you must still keep most of your SSP records.

You can demand full *medical reports*, but employees must be informed that they have a right to approve or amend the report or, having seen it, to refuse to supply it, unless it refers to a third party. The doctor is entitled to refuse to make amendments or to permit disclosure on the ground that it would prejudice the employee's health.

If you suspect malingering, the Revenue will assist, provided the employee has been off sick for four or more short periods in 12 months. A letter to the local HMRC (NICs) office with a report from the employee's doctor may persuade it to ask for a medical examination. HMRC will send the result of the examination to you stating whether there are reasonable grounds for the absences or whether the employee is incapable of work. If the employee is capable of work, you must decide whether or not to continue paying SSP. The same applies if the employee refused to disclose a doctor's report. If you stop the payments at this stage, the employee is entitled to hear your reasons for doing so. If requested, you must give a written explanation and the employee can seek the Revenue's formal decision as to entitlement to SSP.

Trade unions

Employees can belong to any union even if it is not the union with sole representational rights. Payment of subscriptions must be authorised by members at least once every three years and employees can participate in TU activities as agreed with you or as provided in the union membership agreement.

The 2004 Employment Relations Act has made it easier for trade unions to achieve recognition and meet statutory balloting and notification requirements. Some provisions are intended to prevent employers from offering inducements or subjecting employees to a detriment in order to avoid collective bargaining.

The rules for industrial action ballots and ballot notices have been eased and employees taking official and lawfully organised industrial action now have increased protection. Unions are entitled to expel members whose political behaviour is incompatible with union membership, eg members engaged in racist activities.

Union members must not be penalised for using the union's services. They are entitled to a companion at grievance and disciplinary hearings and to be informed and consulted on management decisions affecting their future.

You are entitled to at least seven days' written notice of official industrial action, to assist you in making plans and bringing information to the attention of employees. The union does not have to name the employees involved. After notice has been given and before action is taken, there must be a postal ballot of members. It is no longer unlawful if an individual who was denied a vote is called on to join the strike.

The union does not have to give further notice if continuous industrial action is suspended and then resumed.

Unions are not responsible for members' unofficial activities but they are liable for interference leading to breach of commercial contracts unless industrial action is in contemplation or furtherance of a trade dispute. They cannot bring in outsiders and picketing is only permitted at or near the employees' place of work. You may be able to bring proceedings if industrial action is unlawful.

Works Councils provide a formal framework for consultation between employers and workers' representatives. Legislation introducing Works Councils into our law, however, only applies to organisations with at least 1,000 employees across the EU or at least 150 in each of two or more member states.

Anti-discrimination legislation

You must not discriminate against full- or part-time employees because of colour, race, ethnic or national origin, sex, sexual orientation or marital status, age, their disability or their religious or other beliefs.

But you can insist on employing men or women for specific jobs if their sex is a genuine occupational qualification, it is justified by the nature or circumstances of the job, or the employee is required to work or live in a private home.

Women and men are entitled to be paid the same if doing the same or equivalent work, although economic factors affecting the business may justify paying different wages when they are not employed contemporaneously. They must also be treated in the same way in relation to employee-related benefit and occupational pension schemes.

Statutory Maternity Pay (SMP) and maternity leave and maternity allowance

All pregnant employees with 26 weeks' continuous employment at the beginning of the fourteenth week before the baby is due can claim 26 weeks' Statutory Maternity Pay (SMP) from you, the employer, even if they do not intend to return to work, provided their average weekly gross earnings are not less than £84. Payments are at a rate of 90 per cent of average weekly earnings for the first six weeks and £108.85 or, if less, 90 per cent of average weekly earnings for the remaining 20 weeks. Pay during additional maternity absence from the end of the statutory period to the end of the twenty-eighth week after the birth is subject to agreement, and return to work can be postponed for another four weeks because of illness or another proper reason.

If employees have 26 weeks' continuous employment by the beginning of the fourteenth week before the baby is due they can claim 26 weeks' additional maternity leave. This is usually unpaid, unless the employee has contractual rights. If employees cannot then return to work because of redundancy, they must be offered suitable alternative employment.

Registered self-employed employees paying Class 1 NICs or holding a Small Earnings Exception certificate (see page 99) can claim Maternity Allowance (MA). They must have worked for you for at least 26 weeks of the 'test period' (ie 66 weeks up to and including the week before the baby is due) and earn an average of £30 in any 13 weeks in the test period. MA pays a standard weekly rate of £98.85 or 90 per cent of average weekly earnings before tax, whichever is the smaller; it is not subject to tax or NICs and is not paid during periods of work.

Employees must notify and confirm the pregnancy, and you can claim reimbursement of 92 per cent of SMP from the total amount of employees' and employers' NICs due to the HMRC Accounts Office.

Small Employers' Relief (SER) of 100 per cent of the SMP paid plus 4.5 per cent of the amount as compensation is available if you pay or are liable to pay total employers' and employees' gross Class 1 NICs that do not exceed £45,000. If you pay contracted-out NICs, you should deduct your contracted-out rebate from your employer's NICs when calculating whether or not you qualify. Class 1A NICs on company cars and Class 1B NICs PAYE Settlement Agreements are not included.

Records must be kept on HMRC forms, magnetic tape or in computerised form and retained for at least three years. Other forms can be obtained from your Social Security office, but problems are referred to HMRC. Payments must be noted on employees' Deduction Working Sheets (P11) and End of Year Returns (P14) and on your annual statement, declaration and certificate (P35).

Statutory paternity pay (SPP) and paternity leave

Female and male employees who have worked for 26 continuous weeks prior to the fifteenth week before a baby is due and who are not taking adoption leave (see below) can claim up to two consecutive weeks' paternity leave.

'Father' includes the biological father and the mother's husband or partner living in an enduring family relationship, as well as the adoptive parents.

Employees must notify you of the intention to take this leave in the fifteenth week before the baby is due. You must provide a self-certificate for them to complete with details, and you must respond within 28 days. Leave must be taken within 56 days of the birth or placement for adoption, or from a fixed period or date after the baby is expected.

Statutory parternity pay (SPP) is claimed at the same rate and on the same basis as SMP, but is not payable if the employee receives SSP.

Statutory adoption pay (SAP) and adoption leave

Adoptive parents employed continuously for 26 weeks prior to the date they are matched with a child can take 26 weeks' ordinary adoption leave plus 26 weeks' additional adoption leave. Leave starts from the date the child is placed or from a fixed date up to 14 days before placement.

Adopters must tell you they intend to take the leave, and give details of the placement date and start of leave within seven days of being notified they have been matched for adoption. You must respond within 28 days with the date they are due to return to work. The adopters can change the start of leave on 28 days' written notice.

Either parent can claim but leave cannot be split between them. Male and female adopters can opt instead to take paternity leave.

Statutory adoption pay (SAP) is claimed at the same rate and on the same basis as SMP, but is not payable if the employee receives SSP.

Disabled employees

You must not discriminate against disabled persons, including people with HIV, cancer, multiple sclerosis and visual or other impairment. As with other anti-discrimination legislation, it is unlawful to refuse to offer disabled employees work or to treat them less favourably than other employees. They are entitled to additional training and time off for treatment during working hours. If practicable, you may have to provide special or modified equipment.

If you have more than 20 employees 3 per cent of the workforce must be registered disabled unless the work is dangerous.

Employees with criminal records

Apart from caring services and some professions, employees need not disclose some fines, court orders and custodial sentences of over 6 months 'spent' after periods of up to 10 years. Life imprisonment and preventive detention cannot be 'spent'. Dismissal for failure to disclose unspent convictions is fair.

Exposure to health risks

After working for four weeks employees can claim up to 26 weeks' pay if exposed to some health risks, unless they are unable to work or unreasonably refuse alternative work.

Guarantee and redundancy payments

Unless they are seasonal or casual workers, apprentices, over retirement age or have given written notice under a contract of at least two years, there is a trade dispute or they unreasonably refuse alternative work, employees with you for four weeks can claim guarantee payments after 12 weeks without work for every day without work. The maximum claim is £19.60 for a maximum of five days in a three-month period unless there is a collective agreement.

Redundancy payments can be claimed when lay-off or short-time work lasts for more than four weeks or more than 6 in 13 and employees have received less than half a week's pay. You can agree to pay or, by counter-notice in response to a request, state that you reasonably expect to be able to provide at least 13 weeks' continuous work and if there is then no work the employee is entitled to payments. Employees redundant after two years' continuous work can claim even if they volunteer for redundancy or immediately find other employment. Claims must be made within six months and are as follows:

- half a week's pay for employees between 18 and 22 up to the age of 21;
- a week's pay for employees over 22 up to the age of 40;
- one and a half week's pay for employees aged 41 and over;

for each year of employment. Pay includes overtime plus payment for one week's notice for every complete year worked to a maximum of 12 weeks. The maximum entitlement is for 20 years at £310 per week for 20 weeks. There is no liability to tax or NICs for payments up to £30,000. An employee given notice of redundancy by agreement still qualifies for payment but the notice period must have started by the date on which the employee leaves. Payment must be made when dismissal occurs or soon after.

If independent trade union members are affected, you must consult their representatives before dismissal, giving reasons and stating how many and which employees are to be made redundant. You must do all you can to comply with the requirements if there is insufficient time for full consultation.

Directors or shareholders can authorise additional payments for employees when a company is taken over or wound up.

Employees' obligations

The law assumes that employer and employees enjoy each other's trust and confidence. Employees must follow lawful and reasonable orders and take proper care of your property and must not disclose your industrial and trade secrets unless required to do so by the law.

These belong to the employer if made in the course of employment. Employees should sign agreements to protect you against disclosure of confidential information and from competition but the courts will not enforce one which effectively stops them making a living and you cannot stop disclosure to the Revenue or FIMBRA. If you repudiate the agreement, you cannot enforce the restrictions put on the employee.

References

You do not have to supply references. An employee can sue on a bad reference, but there is no claim if it is true and made without malice (see also page 191, Data Protection). If the reference is too favourable, you may be liable to a new employer if the employee is unsatisfactory.

Inducing breach of the contract of employment

Persuading someone to leave a job is actionable by the ex-employer as an inducement to breach of contract.

Disciplinary powers of management

Some disciplinary powers are specified under the employment and earlier legislation. Procedures should be fair and worked out with the employees and their representatives. Employees should know who can take action and in what circumstances. They must have an opportunity to defend themselves and a right to appeal to a senior level of management or independent arbitration. Fines can only be imposed for breaches of discipline likely to cause loss and must be fair and reasonable. Deductions from pay can be made in connection with disciplinary proceedings under statute. Procedures should be set out in a rule book and employees should acknowledge agreement by signature. Details should also be included in contracts of employment or notices and, unless based on trade practice, in collective agreements.

Statutory grievance and disciplinary procedures must be written into all employment contracts; breach constitutes breach of contract and unfair dismissal. The procedure can be found on the ACAS website.

Codes of practice

Some disciplinary powers and procedures are set out in codes of practice issued under the employment legislation. These codes under the health and safety legislation, the anti-discrimination legislation and TUC codes that cover trade disputes and payments to political funds can be obtained from the ACAS website on www.ACAS.org.uk/publications/pdf/cop.pdf and HMSO on www.hmso.gov.uk. The codes do not have the force of law but are taken into consideration in the event of disputes.

Retirement

The national 'default retirement age' is now 65. Unless you have a legitimate business reason compulsory retirement before that age is unlawful. You can, however, agree on another age for retirement, provided it apples to **all** employees.

Employees given notice they are to be retired at 65 or the agreed retirement age before April 2007 must be notified in writing that they are to cease work on the date specified in their contract or after the four weeks' statutory notice period. They must also be informed they are entitled to ask to continue working. Their written request to do so must be made as soon as reasonably practicable and in any event four weeks before the intended retirement date or not more than four weeks after termination. They are entitled to meet you to discuss the request within a reasonable time and can bring someone with them for support.

If disciplinary and grievance procedures are not reasonably justified, you may face a claim for unfair dismissal.

Dismissal

The unfair dismissal provisions apply to full-time and part-time employees who have worked for you for a year, except those working or residing abroad.

There is no one-year qualifying period and dismissal and redundancy is unfair for the following 'inadmissible' reasons:

- ▨ sex, race or other discrimination;
- ▨ using or attempting to exercise a statutory right, eg taking maternity leave;
- ▨ unjustified dismissal of an employee over retirement age;
- ▨ non-compliance with Sunday employment legislation;
- ▨ for taking appropriate action on health or safety grounds – selection for redundancy on this ground is also unfair dismissal;
- ▨ TU membership or TU activities.

You can fairly dismiss employees on strike on written notice stating if they do not return to work with a specified time they will be dismissed and the dismissal is during the strike.

If disciplinary grievance procedures do not comply with statutory guidelines employees can claim unfair dismissal and the award can be increased by up to 50 per cent.

Employees employed for less than a year, or who suffer a detriment, eg demotion, whatever their age, or are dismissed or made redundant after jury service or after being summoned for jury service may also have a claim for unfair dismissal. *And* dismissal of employees employed for less than a year whatever their age on a refusal of a flexible working hours application or other working parents' rights without following the statutory procedure is automatically unfair.

Retail shop employees must be given a written statement setting out their rights in connection with Sunday work within two months of engagement. They cannot be dismissed or penalised for refusing to work on Sundays if this was agreed at the outset or if they agreed before 26 August 1994 to work Sundays. If Sunday work is agreed, the employee can give later written notice of objection which is usually effective after three months.

Fair dismissal is based on one of the following:

- the employee's capabilities or qualifications (*if* required by the contract);
- misconduct – eg persistent drunkenness or dishonesty;
- redundancy – 'Last in first out' (LIFO) is usually safest and fairest;
- the employee cannot continue work without breaking the law – eg a driver loses his driving licence;
- some other substantial reason – eg going into business in competition with you;
- on transfer of the business: for economic, technical or organisational reasons (see page 240).

Putting an employee in an untenable position, thereby compelling him or her to resign – eg moving a senior executive into a very small office although paying the same salary – may be unfair and also wrongful dismissal.

You must act fairly and reasonably and the employee must have a chance to defend him- or herself. Instant dismissal is rarely justified and warnings, if possible written, should be given, with details of the complaint and stating that dismissal will follow if there is no improvement. Usually you must give a second written warning before you can consider suspension or dismissal. Reasons for dismissal must be sent to the employee within 14 days of dismissal.

If unfair, an industrial tribunal will, if practicable, order reinstatement in the same job, re-engagement in a similar job, or compensation which consists of a basic award of half a week's pay to one-and-a-half weeks' pay at a maximum of £310 per week for each year of employment, depending on age and length of service for a maximum of 30 weeks, with a maximum of £9,300.

The minimum basic award for dismissal on trade union, health and safety, occupational pension scheme trustee, employee representative and working time grounds is £4,200. For employees excluded or expelled from a trade union and not admitted or re-admitted by the date of a tribunal application this is increased to £6,600.

There is in addition an award of £2,700 for unlawful inducement relating to trade union membership, activities or services and for unlawful inducement relating to collective bargaining.

The maximum compensatory award considered 'just and equitable' in the circumstances is £60,000, but there is no limit if the employee was unfairly dismissed or made redundant because of health and safety concerns or public interest disclosure ('whistleblowing').

If the tribunal's order for reinstatement or re-engagement is ignored or if dismissal is for sex, or racial, or other discrimination, an additional award of between 26 and 52 weeks' pay at a maximum of £310 per week to a maximum of £16,120 may be ordered.

Part of the compensatory award in unfair dismissal cases compensates an employee for loss of earnings to the date of the tribunal hearing. The employee may, however, have already received unemployment benefit or income support for this period. The tribunal will therefore order the employer to pay a specified amount of the employee's award to the Jobcentre Plus to avoid 'double payment' to the employee.

The employee must mitigate his or her loss and seek alternative employment and the amount may be reduced if the employee unreasonably refuses reinstatement, has found other work, or conduct was a contributory factor.

If the employee loses, he or she does not have to pay your legal costs unless the tribunal decide the allegations were serious or unfounded, but you may be able to obtain payment of all or some of your costs if the dismissal was because of TU pressure.

The tribunal can also award damages for breach of the employment contract of up to £25,000.

E-mail and your employees

If your employees have agreed that you can monitor their e-mails, you can legally dismiss them for sending and receiving e-mails that do not relate to their work. You need their specific agreement, preferably under a clause in the statement or contract of employment that gives you the right to monitor all messages created, sent, received and stored on your systems, or a clause stating they are not the employees' private property and there should be no expectation of privacy.

Your right to monitor employees' e-mails may conflict with the Data Protection Act 1998, and possibly also with the implied contractual relationship of mutual confidence and trust between employer and employee, and employees' right to privacy under the Human Rights Act 1998. Your best course therefore is to agree sensible guidelines on good business practice and guidelines to safeguard employees' privacy and your business interests, to include an appropriate consent clause in individual statements and contracts of employment, and to follow the Employment Practices Data Protection Code.

The code sets out helpful guidelines about complying with data protection provisions, and covers all 'electronic communications', that is, e-mails, faxes, telephone calls, internet access and CCTV and audio surveillance, but not records kept in response to specific queries, such as customer complaints. It assumes monitoring is intrusive and advises that advantage should be weighed against its impact on employees. Anyone with access to personal data should be aware of the data protection requirements and should be identified to employees, and third parties who contact employees should be told about monitoring.

Only the address and header information of e-mails should be checked unless it is essential to monitor content. Covert monitoring is only justified in exceptional circumstances, such as if fraud is suspected.

Employees should:

▨ be told when they will be monitored, the justification, how the information will be used and to whom disclosed;
▨ have written details if the information is to be used in disciplinary procedures;

- ■ be able to comment on the information before action is taken;
- ■ know how long the information is kept.

Wrongful dismissal

If you break a term of the individual contract of employment the employee can claim damages for wrongful dismissal in the civil courts under the general law which may amount to far more than compensation for unfair dismissal. Damages here are based on what the employee loses and expects to lose by instant unemployment and he or she must seek comparable alternative employment to minimise loss. If the employee instead chooses to take a claim to the employment tribunal, the maximum amount of an award for breach of contract is £25,000.

But whether the claim is unfair and/or wrongful dismissal, you cannot be forced to take an employee back and you always have the choice of paying compensation instead.

Offences and penalties

It is a criminal offence to refuse to pay the minimum wage, fail to keep proper records or to obstruct officers making enquiries under the legislation. There are fines of up to £5,000 for failing to pay and keep records of SMP and SSP, and for failing to provide information related to claims for SMP, SSP, AP, Incapacity Benefit, Maternity Allowance or Severe Disablement Allowance, plus a daily fine until you have put things right. A heavier fine or three months' imprisonment is the additional penalty for knowingly providing, or allowing to be provided, false documents or information relating to claims and compensation. Fines are also imposed for non-compliance with the anti-discrimination legislation.

Blowing the whistle

'Whistleblowers' who report a deliberate cover-up of any of the following are now protected against unfair dismissal and other sanctions:

- a crime or breach of a statutory obligation;
- a miscarriage of justice;
- danger to health and safety or the environment.

The self-employed and voluntary workers are not covered.
  Protection only extends to:

- a reasonable, if not necessarily correct, belief at the time of disclosure;
- information passed to the employer or someone specified in the employer's internal procedure;
- information passed to a third party reasonably believed to be solely or mainly responsible for the wrongdoing;
- information passed to a legal adviser when obtaining legal advice.

To obtain protection for wider disclosures, such as to the police, media or MPs, the employee must either:

- give substantially the same information;
- reasonably believe he or she would be victimised if the disclosure were made internally;
- reasonably believe the evidence is likely to be suppressed or destroyed if disclosure is made internally.

Alternatively the wrongdoing must be exceptionally serious, the employee must not act for personal gain, and he or she must act reasonably, particularly in regard to:

- deciding to whom to disclose;
- the seriousness of the wrongdoing;
- whether the risk or danger continues;
- the reasonableness of the employer's response to a previous disclosure;
- whether the employee complied or should have complied with internal procedure;
- whether disclosure breaches the employee duty of confidentiality.

You cannot prohibit 'protected' disclosures by a clause in an employment contract or severance agreement.

Dismissal after whistleblowing is treated as automatically unfair, and a victimised employee can claim compensation for the loss suffered and expenses reasonably incurred. Protection extends to post-employment victimisation, eg denying a whistleblower a reference. You are therefore advised to have a whistleblowing policy that encourages confidential internal disclosure.

Human rights in the workplace

Individual rights protected by the Human Rights Act could be breached if:

■ there is sexual or racial discrimination, or discrimination on the ground of sexual orientation;
■ there is use of CCTV and monitoring of e-mail and phone calls;
■ employees cannot practise their religion because of the demands of work;
■ employees are bound by contractual confidentiality clauses.

An employer may be able to justify apparent breaches of these areas, but justification must be genuine and impingement of the right must go no further than is required to achieve the stated purpose.

Statutory references

Access to Medical Reports Act 1988
Companies Act 1985
Contracts of Employment Act 1972
Copyright, Designs and Patents Act 1988
Data Protection Act 1998
Deregulation and Contracted Out Act 1994
Disability Discrimination Acts 1995 and 2005
Employment Acts 1980, 1982, 1989, 1990 and 2002

Employment of Children Act 1973
Employment Protection Act 1975
Employment Protection (Consolidation) Act 1978
Employment Relations Act 1999 and 2004
Employment Rights Act 1996
Employment Subsidies Act 1978
Equal Pay Act 1970
Factories Act 1961
Health and Safety at Work Act 1974
Human Rights Act 1998
Industrial Tribunals Act 1996
National Minimum Wage (Enforcement Notices) Act 2003
Public Interest Disclosure Act 1998
Race Relations Act 1976
Regulatory Investigative Powers Act 2000
Regulation of Investigatory Powers Act 2000
Rehabilitation of Offenders Act 1974
Sex Discrimination Acts 1975 and 1986
Social Security Acts 1975 and 1989
Social Security Contributions and Benefits Act 1992
Sunday Trading Act 1994
Trade Union and Labour Relations (Consolidation) Act 1992
Trade Union Reform and Employment Rights Act 1993
Wages Act 1986

9

Trading

This chapter covers the law of sale of goods and consumer credit, which affect the day-to-day search for profits. Like the law of landlord and tenant and insurance, they are based on contract law.

Contracts

Contracts are agreements between willing parties who exchange promises, eg a promise to deliver goods in return for a promise to pay. The promises *plus* implied terms make up the contract and contract law dictates the remedies for non-performance.

Theoretically, and with important exceptions, oral contracts are as good as written ones but it is better and safer to incorporate business arrangements into written contracts.

Some agreements, including some leases and business contracts, must be written and state that the document is intended to be a deed and both parties must sign (execute) it. One witness is sufficient unless signing on behalf of someone else (eg a company), when there must be two. Sealing, ie sticking a red seal at the foot of the document, is only necessary when required by a company's Articles but the deed must be delivered (handed over).

Only the parties are liable under the contract but agents can pass liability to a principal (as directors do with the company).

Third parties, however, can now claim the same rights and remedies as the contracting parties if the contract specifically gives them rights or if it was made for their benefit. The third party must be identifiable by name or description, and may have to share rights and remedies with a contracting party. If they have rights, they cannot be deprived of them without their consent unless the contract provides for it. There are, however, no third party rights in employment contracts, contracts for the carriage of goods and contracts relating to negotiable instruments (that is, cheques, bills of exchange, etc – see pages 164–69).

Contracts for business abroad made via e-mail may be governed by foreign law. They should therefore state they are governed by English law for convenience, speed and to save costs. Otherwise where the case is heard may have to be decided in accordance with the Rome Convention. And you may have to pursue judgment through foreign courts anyway, if there is no property here to satisfy the claim.

Arbitration

You can agree to have disputes settled by arbitration or mediation. There may be considerable savings in costs, particularly in landlord and tenant and commercial disputes. Information is available from the Centre for Effective Dispute Resolution (CEDR) (see page 246 for contact details).

Buying and selling for cash

If goods are sold for cash the transaction is governed by the sale of goods legislation and the custom of the trade.

Business buyers have partial protection. They can safely assume the seller owns the goods and the parties cannot be totally unreasonable – a seller with a monopoly will probably be unable to exclude the statutory quality guarantee.

Consumers have full protection: goods must be of satisfactory quality, fit for the purposes for which goods of that kind are commonly supplied, taking into account the price and other relevant circumstances. 'Quality' includes:

- the state and condition of the goods;
- appearance and finish;
- safety and durability;

and they must be free from minor defects except for defects:

- drawn to the buyer's attention;
- discoverable on inspection, if the buyer was given a chance to inspect them;
- apparent on reasonable inspection of a sample in sale by sample.

And they must correspond with samples, descriptions and display items. The protection covers some agreements to hire goods and contracts for services, including repairs and maintenance where work must be done in a reasonable time, with reasonable care and skill and, if no price is agreed, at a reasonable price.

Consumer contracts must be in 'plain intelligible language' and 'unfair' terms are unlawful and void, which here means contrary to good faith and significantly weighting the contract against the consumer. The consumer can now, for instance, sue directly on a penalty clause even if the contract states that he or she has no right to do so.

Selling to consumers can bring liability for others' mistakes, eg for inadequate manufacturer's instructions.

Liability for quality and quantity can be restricted or excluded but the law more readily permits a limitation of liability. Only specific wording excludes liability for negligence or non-performance and in dealing with consumers the clause or notice on your premises has no legal effect. Widely framed indemnity clauses are illegal and you are liable for accidents resulting in personal injury or death. But liability for financial loss and damage can be restricted if the contractual clause or notice is reasonable in the circumstances. Here the bargaining strength of the parties and the price are relevant in business transactions and consumers have more protection.

Importer, manufacturer, packager, carrier, installer, distributor, retailer, hirer and anyone putting names or labels on goods is strictly (automatically) liable to consumers for death, personal injury and loss or damage to property exceeding £275. Defences include compliance with the law or scientific and technical knowledge, and liability can be passed up and down the chain of supply. Personal injury claims must be made within three years of the date the claimant knew his rights; a six-year time limit applies to contractual claims. No claim can be made after products have been circulated for 10 years.

A manufacturer's guarantee cannot limit liability for negligence or exclude or restrict the consumer's contractual rights.

In commercial transactions you can agree almost anything you like but there are legal limits. The following clauses are void:

- contravention of EU law;
- excluding or restricting liability for personal injury or death due to negligence;
- excluding or restricting implied terms as to title and in consumer contracts restricting implied terms as to description, quality and fitness;
- excluding or restricting liability in guarantees for loss or damage arising from defective consumer goods due to negligence in manufacture or distribution.

In deciding if a term is unfair to consumers, all the relevant circumstances at the time the contract was concluded are taken into account, including the nature of the goods and services. And the following clauses are subject to the 'reasonableness' test:

- attempts to exclude or restrict liability for negligence causing loss or damage;
- attempts to exclude or restrict liability for breach of contract;
- attempts to entitle a party to provide a contractual performance substantially different from that reasonably expected;
- attempts to provide no performance if one party is a consumer or contracts on the other party's standard terms;
- attempts to require a consumer to indemnify someone else for liability for negligence or breach of contract;
- negligence causing loss or damage.

Agreeing the contract

First comes the offer. When a firm offer is accepted, the contract is complete. Accepting a specific quantity of specific goods delivered over a fixed period at a fixed price is acceptance of the whole consignment, even if delivered by instalments. A buyer can revoke a contract for a maximum quantity as and when demanded. It is basically a standing offer, each order being placed under a separate contract but goods already ordered must be accepted.

Acceptance by post is received when posted even if not received. Oral, faxed and (presumably, there are no cases on it) e-mailed acceptance is received when heard or seen. Offers to sell can be cancelled any time before being accepted but should be confirmed before selling elsewhere. Acceptance varying an offer – eg by asking for a different quantity – may be a counter-offer, requiring the other side's acceptance. If you do not ask for formal acceptance, goods are accepted unless rejected within a reasonable time or they form part of a 'commercial unit' (see below) but not if a buyer asks for or has agreed to repair or has re-sold them.

Standard terms of business in consumer transactions must be intelligible and consumers can refer to the courts to assess fairness. Business customers are less protected and if both parties use standard terms – eg in order forms and delivery notes – each set may be a counter-offer. The contract may then incorporate the terms of the last document exchanged but unusual or onerous terms are only incorporated if specifically pointed out.

Payment and delivery

The law will not put a whole contract together. Terms of the trade or terms included in previous dealings may be incorporated but if price, quality, size, style and design or content are not agreed, there may be no contract unless omissions are minor details. If price is not agreed, the buyer must pay a 'reasonable' price within a reasonable time. Deposits are usually lost if the buyer does not complete the transaction but part payments must be returned.

The right to claim (statutory) interest at 8 per cent above current bank base rate on debts for goods and services supplied to other traders is now automatically incorporated into business contracts. Interest becomes due the day after the specified date for payment, or the 30th day after delivery, or the 30th day after the purchaser is notified of the debt – whichever is the later.

A contractual term excluding statutory interest is void unless you have agreed a term allowing interest on late payments at a reasonable and substantial rate.

Unless otherwise agreed, you can take delivery when you pay. If nothing is agreed, the law spells out the details as follows:

■ You can refuse delivery of more or less than ordered, unless the amount is negligible. If accepted you must pay, *pro rata*, at the contract price.
■ If goods are mixed with goods not ordered, you can accept all the goods or only those ordered.
■ You can reject all or part of a consignment, including goods under an instalment contract, which does not conform with the contract, *unless* part of a 'commercial unit' and division would impair the goods' value or character – eg parts of a machine – but you may be able to exclude this provision in business transactions.

And you do not have to return rejected goods, although you must notify the seller of rejection.

Payment, unless otherwise agreed, is not due until delivery but if goods are lost or destroyed while at your risk, you may have to pay for them. When you pay, the seller must deliver or pay damages. If unique goods – eg antiques – are involved, the court will order delivery whatever the cost.

If the price is not paid or offered, the seller can retain goods, stop them in transit or sell them elsewhere. After delivery to a carrier, delivery can only be held up if the right has been expressly reserved, unless the carrier is an independent middleman. Delivery of instalment contracts cannot be held up to extract payment for earlier deliveries.

The owner takes the risk and a buyer may own goods before receiving and paying for them. A clause providing goods remain the seller's until paid for – a 'retention of title clause' – protects a seller if a buyer becomes insolvent. This is relatively straightforward for intact goods but provisions covering sale proceeds or materials to be mixed or processed with other goods should be professionally drafted. You may also have to register a charge on the buyer's assets in the Register of Bills of Sale or with the Companies Registry to preserve priority in insolvency.

Ownership passes from seller to buyer as stated expressly or by inference from the contract or surrounding circumstances. If the question is still open ownership depends on whether goods are:

- 'specific' – identified and agreed at the time of the contract;
- 'unascertained' – bought from bulk or of a particular type – eg 12 clocks from stock or 12 clocks.

Goods can also be 'ascertained' by 'exhaustion', for example your purchase of 600 crates of beer sent to you by lorry carrying a consignment of 1,000 crates is yours as soon as the carrier off-loads 400 crates.

Similarly, if you order a quarter of a bulk consignment, eg 8,000 litres of oil, brought to you by tanker, provided the contract of sale identifies your order, you own 2,000 litres of the oil as soon as you have paid for it.

The law then makes the following rules regarding ownership for specific goods:

- if finished and in a deliverable state – the buyer's when the offer is accepted;
- if put into a deliverable state – eg by weighing – the buyer's when notified they are ready to deliver;
- if in the process of construction/manufacture – the buyer's when materials are set aside and identified;
- if held on sale or return – when agreed or accepted, otherwise the buyer's within a reasonable time.

Future or unascertained goods in a deliverable state sold by description are the buyer's when handed to him or her or a carrier or put in storage.

These rules are contractual only and do not apply to negligence claims.

Misrepresentation

When you are deliberately misled you may be able to claim damages plus reimbursement from the seller, but you must prove the misrepresentation persuaded you to close the deal. You can usually cancel if the seller is careless or genuinely mistaken unless you have agreed to accept the goods or a third party is involved but a specifically worded clause can restrict or exclude liability.

Criminal offences

It is an offence to apply false trade descriptions (FTDs) to goods, or to supply, or offer to supply, goods to which one has been applied. This covers almost any oral or written statement as to quantity, size, manufacture, production, composition, fitness for the purpose, strength, performance and other physical characteristics, testing and approval; previous ownership and other history and dishonesty do not have to be proved. Liability can be disclaimed by an effective disclaimer specifically brought to the buyer's attention.

The provisions also cover a private seller's oral statements and descriptions of services and accommodation, unfair pricing and misleading indications of British origin. You can be vicariously liable for an employee's FTD if you knew it was false when made or read.

A false representation in words or conduct with the intent to make a gain or cause loss or risk to another is also an offence under the Fraud Act 2006.

Local weights and measures authorities can make test purchases, enter premises and seize goods but usually issue proceedings only if there is a public need for protection. If you are trading for profit you can bring civil proceedings for injunctions to restrain a competitor's further wrongful acts, and you can claim damages and costs.

It is an offence to make, or not correct, uninformative or misleading bargain offers for foods, services, accommodation and facilities (other than investment business).

Misleading advertising

The Director of Fair Trading takes action to stop publication of misleading advertisements for goods and services. The IBA and cable authorities cover commercial TV, radio and cable TV, and traders can be ordered to withdraw advertisements making false claims about food.

Buying and selling on credit

The 1974 and 2006 Consumer Credit Acts and associated legislation apply to credit arrangements for amounts exceeding £50, excluding interest and including optional charges and insurance – other than life insurance premiums for loans secured on land. *But* existing credit agreements within the £25,000 previous statutory limit are unaffected.

The sum of £25,000 continues to be the limit for a loan entered into by an 'individual', ie a sole trader or partner in a partnership of less than four partners, if it is 'wholly or predominantly' for business purposes and the agreement includes a declaration to that effect. The declaration will, however, be ineffective if the creditor, or someone acting on his or her behalf, eg a broker, knew or had reasonable cause to suspect that the agreement was not being entered into for business purposes.

Unless agreed otherwise, the agreement between lender and dealer is covered by the sale of goods legislation.

The £25,000 limit does not apply to company borrowings, or loans to partnerships with more than three partners. And credit arrangements with banks, exempt lenders and companies with a capital of over £250 million with a specialised banking service are not covered by the consumer credit legislation. Except for EU central banks and exempt lenders, banks must be licensed and comply with banking legislation. No statutory credit can be charged in connection with a credit or security agreement.

Debtors with a 'high net worth', ie with earnings or assets over a currently unidentified threshold can opt out of the legislation provided the creditor obtains a 'statement of high net worth' for the debtor from an appropriately qualified third party. As from 6 April 2007 new agreements with unfair or oppressive terms can be set aside by the court and the creditor, or his or her associate, may be ordered to vary the terms or repay some or all of the amounts paid.

The consumer credit legislation is still in the process of being amended. Some provisions of the 2006 Act will not come into force until 2007 or 2008 and some are subject to consultation.

Anyone advising on credit terms must have a licence. Licences are available from the Office of Fair Trading and valid for five years at a cost of £110 for sole traders and £275 for partnerships and companies. The Office must be notified of changes affecting the licence – eg new business premises or a change of partners or directors – within 21 days. It is an offence to trade without a licence and unlicensed advisers cannot enforce the agreement, although the borrower can do so. There will be a new licensing regime from 6 April 2008.

It is also an offence to send out unsolicited credit cards or circulars about credit to anyone under 18. Unsolicited cash loans can only be offered at the lender's business premises.

Consumer credit and hire agreements can be concluded online and copies of agreements and notices can be sent out electronically. Borrowers are entitled to have details of their credit references and as from 8 April 2008 regular information about the state of their account, including notice of arrears and notices of default. If two consecutive payments are unpaid, they must be sent 'early warning' notice. Additional information is likely to be necessary in current running-account statements, eg credit card statements, warning customers about the dangers of making minimum payments and missing payments.

The creditor is only entitled to simple, not compound, interest on amounts in default. No interest can be charged if the debtor has not received an annual statement for fixed amount and fixed-term loans and hire purchase, conditional sale and credit sale agreements. This provision applies to existing as well as new agreements.

Borrowers are entitled to have details of their credit references.

With hire purchase, you hire goods with an option to purchase. They remain the seller's until the option is exercised. Conditional sale and credit sale agreements are contracts for the sale of goods at a price paid in instalments. In conditional sales, the borrower owns the goods when all payments are made. In credit sales, he or she owns them as soon as the contract is made.

Hire purchase and conditional sales are covered by the 1974 Act. Sale of goods legislation applies to credit sales but the rules on acceptance and delivery are the same whether goods are sold on cash or credit.

Most sales on credit are three-cornered: the dealer sells for cash to the lender and the lender sells or hires to the borrower.

The borrower's signed application form is his or her offer to the lender to buy on credit. When the dealer completes it, the form becomes the dealer's offer to sell to the lender. The lender accepts or rejects both offers and is responsible for the quality guarantee because he or she sells directly to the borrower.

'Regulated' agreements under the 1974 Act must be signed by the borrower and by or on behalf of the lender and must contain details of:

- the transaction;
- the cost of the credit;
- the right to pay the debt before the agreed date;
- the right, if any, to cancel and to whom notice of cancellation is given – usually within 5 to 14 days of signing, depending on the type of agreement. This gives the borrower time to consider the transaction.

Cancellation also cancels linked agreements. Items traded in part exchange or their value are returnable within 10 days and if the borrower returns goods, he or she can claim repayment, plus fees or commissions over £1.

The borrower must be given copies of the agreement. If inaccurate the agreement and linked security agreements are enforceable only by court order. In some cases the lender may not be able to enforce it at all.

Special formalities apply to mortgages. The borrower has 14 days to consider the loan which is only enforceable by court order.

If the lender has a right to cancel, notice of cancellation must usually be served on the borrower. The notice must:

- identify the borrower's breach of the agreement, – eg failure to insure goods, so it can be put right;
- state that if it cannot be put right, he or she can pay specified compensation instead;

- set out the consequences of failing to comply with the notice.

And no further action can be taken by the lender for at least seven days.

No notice is required when the borrower is in arrears or exceeds a credit limit if the lender:

- sues for arrears; or
- restricts the borrower's right to draw on credit.

When over a third of the price is paid, the lender can in some cases only enforce the agreement by court order but the borrower can apply to the court for extra time to pay at any time.

Security for the loan should be included in the agreement or in a document to which it refers. If the borrower provides security, there must be a separate agreement in a prescribed form signed by or on behalf of the guarantor or indemnifier, otherwise it is unenforceable without a court order. If security is given by a third party, eg a recourse agreement between lender and a dealer, it does not have to comply with the Acts. Special formalities apply to some security agreements, eg mortgages of goods and assignments of life assurance policies, which are usually only enforceable if the agreement is enforceable, unless an indemnity is for a borrower under the age of 18.

Security and linked agreements are cancelled with the regulated agreement.

Credit buyer's protection

Buyer protection is the same whether you buy for cash or credit but the quality guarantee is backed by the lender. Both dealer and manufacturer are responsible if goods are not checked before delivery.

Legislation is being considered to require credit agreements to use simple language, to enable consumers more readily to understand the cost of paying the debt and to remove financial penalties for paying the debt off early. An alternative dispute resolution scheme for consumer credit disputes is to be provided by the Financial Ombudsman Service by 6 April 2007.

Consumer hire agreements

These are covered by the Acts if the credit is for more than three months and there are at least three instalment payments. If annual payments exceed £300, or the goods are specialised goods for the borrower's business, or they have been leased to someone else, the lender can repossess them without a court order but only if he or she has obtained consent to entry of the premises.

Hiring industrial plant and machinery

Some manufacturers offer their own financing if agreements are outside the financial limits and machinery is often leased. It then remains the manufacturer's or dealer's property and the borrower's cost of hiring is deductible for tax purposes. In credit sales, the borrower owns the goods and can take advantage of capital allowances.

Mortgages

Mortgages are outside the Acts and some other loans are specifically exempted but second mortgages on land obtained by private individuals are covered by the Acts, whatever the amount.

Doorstep selling

Consumers can refuse to pay for unsolicited goods or services delivered to their home address after an unsolicited visit or telephone call. There is a right to cancel within seven days of contracting and to return unsatisfactory goods within seven days of receipt. The trader must serve notice of the right to cancel within seven days of contracting, stating who must be notified, otherwise the agreement is unenforceable although the consumer's rights are unaffected. Notice of cancellation must be in writing and given personally or by post. Consumers need not return goods until repaid unless a written request is received within 21 days but must take reasonable care of them in the interim. Perishable or consumable goods,

goods incorporated into the consumer's property, eg double glazing, or supplied for an emergency need not be returned but the cash price must be paid.

The provisions also cover goods and services other than those discussed at the trader's premises if not usually supplied by him or her and contracts made while on trips organised by the trader away from business premises. Contracts for work and materials for house repair are covered unless linked to a mortgage but the following are excluded:

■ contracts for time share, sale of land and house extensions;
■ food, drink, household consumables;
■ purchases from trade catalogues if there have been continuous dealings between customer and sales representative;
■ some contracts of insurance;
■ investment agreements;
■ contracts for bank deposits.

Hire purchase, conditional sale agreements and credit exceeding £35 are excluded. The Acts cover credit of between £50 and £25,000 for business purposes to individuals and partnerships with fewer than three partners, but there is no protection for credit between £35 and £50.

Mail order

Mail order contracts often have a cancellation clause and buyer protection is the same as in cash sales. Unless goods are retained to compel repayment, they must be handed over on written request but the customer does not have to arrange for their return.

Remedies for non-performance

If goods are unsatisfactory:

■ Consumers under conditional sales agreements can reject them, even after delivery, unless the transaction has been confirmed.

- If covered by the 1974 Act you can cancel – if the cash price is between £100 and £30,000 supplier and lender are jointly liable to repay deposits.
- In retail sales for cash the customer can refuse credit notes and claim repayment.

A negligent carrier is liable to the owner of damaged goods, even if the owner is not consignor or consignee.

Take advice before claiming for non-delivery. Depending on whether goods have 'perished' (deteriorated), been destroyed or have disappeared, the buyer may be able to claim damages or repayment but may have to pay the seller's necessary expenses. If risk has passed to the buyer, the buyer must pay and claim separately for damages.

If goods do not belong to the seller, you may have to hand them to the owner and claim damages. Goods bought through agents can usually be retained but you should take legal advice before asserting your rights.

If a transaction becomes illegal or there was duress or misrepresentation, there may be a right to rescind (cancel) the contract.

In some circumstances a buyer can claim for consequential loss but reasonable steps must be taken to minimise the loss.

Fines and penalties

Traders whose advertisements mislead consumers about the total charge for credit are liable to fines of up to £2,000 and/or imprisonment.

Statutory references

Administration of Justice Act 1985
Arbitration Acts 1950, 1975 and 1979
Banking Act 1979
Bills of Exchange Act 1882
Bills of Sales Acts 1878 to 1882
Companies Act 1985
Competition Act 1980 & 1988
Consumer Arbitration Agreements Act 1988

Consumer Credit Acts 1974 and 2006
Consumer Protection Act 1987
Consumer Safety Act 1978
Contracts (Applicable Law) Act 1990
Contracts (Rights of Third Parties) Act 1999
Deregulation and Contracting Out Act 1994
Fair Trading Act 1973
Fraud Act 2006
Late Payment of Commercial Debts (Interest) Act 1998
Latent Damage Act 1986
Law of Property Act 1925
Law of Property (Miscellaneous Provisions) Act 1989
Law Reform (Frustrated Contracts) Act 1943
Limitation Act 1980
Misrepresentation Act 1967
Sale of Goods Act 1979
Sale of Goods (Amendment) Act 1995
Sale of Goods (Implied Terms) Act 1973
Sale and Supply of Goods Act 1994
Supply of Goods and Services Act 1982
Sunday Trading Act 1994
Supply of Goods (Amendment) Act 1994
Supreme Court Act 1981
Trade Descriptions Acts 1968 and 1972
Unfair Contract Terms Act 1977
Unfair Terms in Consumer Contracts Regulations 1999
Unsolicited Goods and Services Act 1974

10

Cash and credit

Most trading is for cash or credit and your books are debited and credited with money amounts even if you only deal in paper, with rights and a value varying with the content and creditworthiness of the signatories.

You and your bank

Your creditworthiness essentially depends on your bank which must:

- take reasonable care in conducting your business – they are liable for payments on cheques if they are careless or suspect fraud;
- follow your instructions – they are not obliged to warn of any risks inherent in doing so;
- honour cheques to the limit of the account or overdraft – if they refuse, you may be able to claim damages;
- pay you in cash on request;
- not divulge information about you unless compelled by law or the public interest. If a court requires information, they do not have to inform you.

If asked for advice, their duty of care is very limited and can be further limited by disclaimers of liability.

And you must:

■ draw cheques with reasonable care;
■ notify the bank of forgeries.

Opening a bank account

When you open the account, the bank requires references. For partnerships, it requires details of the partners and their authority and involvement in the business and a copy of the partnership agreement. Usually, all the partners sign the mandate (agreement) which sets out assets and liabilities and gives instructions as to the conduct of the account – eg who signs cheques and requests advances – and they must confirm that securities to be held by the bank apply to existing and future liabilities and undertake to notify changes in the partners or the agreement. A sole trader's mandate stands until the account is closed or the business wound up. With partnerships it continues even if the partners or the partnership name changes but incoming partners should confirm its terms and outgoing partners remain liable. Cheques drawn by deceased or bankrupt partners must be approved by the partnership, unless the mandate specifies otherwise.

Opening an LLP or company account is more complicated because of the protection of limited liability. The bank must see the Certificate of Incorporation and the Partnership Agreement, the Memorandum and Articles of Association and a certified copy of the resolution appointing them. The resolution is the company's mandate with the bank and gives instructions about operating the account. Usually the bank supplies a draft resolution to be completed and passed at the first board meeting after arrangements are provisionally agreed. The bank may want a separate resolution covering overdraft facilities, incorporating directors' undertakings given on behalf of the company. The mandate is terminated by board resolution and ends if the account is closed, a receiver appointed, or the company goes into liquidation.

Textile designer

Guitar manufacturer

The similarities can be uncanny.

When you are a part of a worldwide group that serves over 2.5 million business customers of every type and in every sector, you see their similarities as much as their differences. Two apparently different business owners might both prefer to maintain their high standards using personal control. And though their businesses might be growing fast, they both want to make sure that work doesn't take over their lives. Fortunately, with our experience and our range of flexible products, we're in a good position to help you and your business.

For a different perspective on your business, talk to one of our commercial managers today.

Or visit **hsbc.co.uk/business**

COMMERCIAL BANKING

HSBC

The world's local bank

Choosing the right bank

Deciding who to bank with is a crucial decision for small businesses. The relationship with your bank can be fundamental, as it supports you through the challenges of growing and developing your business.

Perhaps the most important thing to look for, over and above any particular feature, is choice. Your bank should adapt to your business, not the other way around; it should free you up rather than tying you down. Here are a few questions to consider. Firstly, how does money flow into and out of your company – in cash, as cheques or electronically? You may want to think about how and when you need to access financial information to assess your cashflow requirement. Another important issue is how you want to deal with your bank, and what kind of support you will need. This will depend on factors such as the nature and age of your company and the level of your in-house financial expertise. And with cost control a key issue for the smaller firm, you also need to think about banking charges and the benefits you'll get for your money.

Accounts

Small businesses need an account that lets them manage their money in a way that suits their individual needs. HSBC's Business Current Account offers everything the typical small business requires. You can make and receive cash, cheques or electronic payments and you're free to manage your account online, by phone or at your local branch at no extra cost. We often have special offers for new account openers, such as free business banking for up to 18 months, discounts on insurance or commercial credit cards without fees for 12 months (terms and conditions apply and account opening is subject to status).

As uncertainty in the job market increases, the idea of a 'job for life' looks more outdated every day. More and more people choose to start up in business to take control of their own careers and futures. The good news is that it's never been easier to take the plunge. Cheaper utilities such as broadband help to level the playing field, allowing smaller firms to compete more effectively than ever before. HSBC plays its part with the Business Direct Account, which could be ideal if you prefer online or telephone banking, don't use cash, receive few cheques and turn over less than £500,000. Best of all, it's completely free within certain transaction limits.

Borrowing

It's a sad fact that many SMEs run into trouble simply because they are under-capitalised – the 'engine' of the business works fine, but there isn't enough financial fuel to keep it running smoothly. The reality is that firms of all sizes need to borrow from time to time, particularly those who hold stock, offer credit or need to invest in premises or equipment. Businesses in the early stages of development and growth often need more cash than they've had time to accumulate, so it's important to think ahead and make a realistic assessment of your borrowing needs.

For day-to-day cashflow management, a traditional business overdraft is often enough. HSBC's overdrafts are easy to arrange – online in some cases – and you pay interest only on each day's balance. It's simple to arrange and could be the ideal choice to manage everyday shortfalls in cashflow due to unexpected purchases or delayed payments. Our Flexible Business Loan is tailored to the needs of your business and offers the choice of fixed or variable interest rates. Options for protection against sickness, accident and death provide additional peace of mind.

Finance solutions

Many SMEs find invoice finance, or 'factoring', invaluable in easing cashflow worries. Essentially this is a way of 'selling' your debts to a bank as soon as invoices are issued, so you release cash, reduce debt and avoid the nightmare of bad debts. If you sell business-to-business on credit terms, factoring could be right for you. You can get an immediate quote online at our website (**www.hsbc.co.uk/1/2/business/finance-borrowing/invoice-finance-factoring**).

The ability to take payments from debit and credit cards is now an essential for any business-to-consumer operation, and for many business-to-business traders. As well as allowing customers to pay for goods and services at the physical point of sale, you may also want to process card details when the cardholder is not present. This opens up the possibilities for taking deposits, selling by mail order, e-commerce, phone ordering and so on. At the end of the day, giving customers the choice to pay how they want can only make them more likely to buy from you.

HSBC's card processing service gives you the ability to accept all major debit and credit cards however they're used – in person, by phone, mail or fax and online. For e-traders, we offer secure internet payments plus fraud management services, online transaction reporting and a multi-currency option.

We also offer a variety of loans which can be tailored to suit your needs.

Insurance

Every business needs some level of insurance. As well as cover for physical assets, you may also need employer's liability insurance, which covers injury to your staff, professional indemnity insurance for claims against the business or trade credit insurance against bad debts. You might also want to insure vehicles, cargo in transit or 'key staff' (people essential to the business). HSBC offers all these and more, including a Small Business Insurance Package, that is tailored specificially to the needs of your business, which also includes a free legal advice helpline. HSBC also understands that your time is precious so everything is done in one simple telephone call with no paper work to complete.

International

The powerful combination of globalisation and technology makes it easy to buy almost anything from almost anywhere. Many businesses now depend on goods and services sourced from overseas, or sell to important clients outside the UK. If you're in this position, you may want to consider having an account in another currency – it's simpler, easier and cheaper than having an account outside the country and reduces your exposure to currency risk. HSBC's International Business Account can be opened in a number of foreign currencies, including euros and US dollars. You can pay suppliers electronically direct from the account and there are options for savings and deposit accounts too.

HSBC Bank plc

HSBC Bank is a wholly-owned subsidiary of HSBC Holdings plc which is headquartered in the UK. The HSBC Group serves over 125 million customers worldwide from more than 9,500 offices in 76 countries and territories in Europe, the Asia-Pacific region, the Americas, the Middle East and Africa. With assets of US$1,738 billion at 30 June 2006, HSBC is one of the world's largest banking and financial services organisations. HSBC is marketed worldwide as 'the world's local bank'.

AC3960.

Guarantees

A guarantee for a sole trader or partner in a partnership of fewer than four partners is covered by the Consumer Credit Acts if it is 'wholly or predominantly' for business purposes. The agreement must include a declaration to that effect, but will be ineffective if the creditor, or someone acting on his or her behalf, eg a broker, knew or had reasonable cause to suspect that it was not a business loan. The guarantees can be open or limited to a fixed amount and become operative when signed by the guarantors. If co-guarantors are insolvent, you can be liable for the whole amount.

Directors' guarantees are not covered by the Consumer Credit Acts.

Bank guarantees commit you to repay any money owed on all your bank accounts for an indefinite period. The guarantee continues until renegotiated but a deceased guarantor's estate may not be liable so co-guarantors should sign on behalf of 'their heirs, executors and administrators'.

Under other guarantees you can turn to the principal debtor and set off anything already paid and you are then entitled to any security given for the debt. Alternatively you or the creditor can sue the debtor or 'prove' – establish your claim – in his or her bankruptcy or liquidation.

The sole trader and partner are liable for all business debts but when company debts are paid, directors are only liable if there are problems with floating charges, or fraudulent preferences, or there has been fraudulent or wrongful trading.

Payments

Your cash and paper are negotiable, ie they give rights and obligations which are transferable. If you hold a negotiable instrument you can sue on it. When you give value in good faith – becoming a 'holder in due course' – it becomes valid even if invalid initially, *provided* it is current, unconditional and appears to be properly completed, unless there is a forgery. Trading via bills of exchange and commercial credits is usually confined to larger businesses, although bills are fairly common in some manufacturing trades and heavy industry. Export business is usually done under letters of credit. Historically and currently a bill of exchange permits a seller to be paid when goods are shipped although the buyer does not pay until they are received or sold elsewhere. The period (tenor) of the bill is usually at least three months, a bank or finance house standing as intermediary for payment, and charging a commission for the advance during the period of transit by discounting the payment. Bills can also be accepted, ie by the acceptor's confirmation that the drawee will pay on the due date. The drawer pays the acceptor an agreed percentage of face value, acceptance is endorsed on the bill, the bill becomes freely negotiable and the acceptor becomes primarily liable to the holder.

The main types of negotiable instruments are:

- bills of exchange – a cheque is a bill;
- promissory notes – which include bank notes;
- bankers' drafts – which can be treated as bills or promissory notes.

Bills of lading – receipts for goods sent by sea – are semi-negotiable; once invalid, they remain invalid. Postal and money orders are not negotiable. Money orders are void 12 months after issue.

Negotiable instruments are promises to pay on a specified date. Banks must stop payment on request but you can be sued on the dishonoured promise to pay and your bank is liable if your cheque is wrongly dishonoured. A formal notice of dishonour is usually sufficient to enforce payment through the court at minimal cost. Defences are very limited and if there is a dispute, the debtor must usually pay up and sue in separate proceedings.

Cheques

A cheque is an unconditional order from you (the drawer) to another (your bank, the drawee) to pay a sum of money on demand to a specified person or 'to bearer':

- If 'to cash or order' it is valid but *not* a cheque because there is no payee.
- Post-dated cheques are valid but banks usually refuse to pay before the due date.
- It is not a continuing security but you remain liable for up to six years (although banks usually return cheques for re-issue after six months).

A cheque crossed 'a/c (or account) payee' with or without 'only' is non-transferable – the crossing can be deleted if you want to transfer it. If you add 'not negotiable' it cannot be negotiated. It can be transferred by endorsement but the endorser cannot pass better title than he or she has him- or herself – a stolen cheque is valueless – and the bank must give notice of dishonour to endorsers.

Unless post-dated, a cheque comes to life when handed over or the payee is told it is held on his or her behalf. The holder is the person to whom it is payable (the payee) or the named endorsee or anyone holding a cheque payable 'to bearer'. The holder can alter the crossing but other alterations without the drawer's consent usually invalidate the cheque. If endorsed after alteration, it is valid for the altered amount against the endorser.

Holders take cheques on the same terms as the payee. But if a cheque is not overdue, the holder gives value in good faith, the cheque is regular on its face and the previous holder was entitled to it, the holder becomes a 'holder in due course'. As a 'holder in due course', he or she is in a stronger position: the cheque can be freely negotiated, payment can be claimed through a non-existent payee and may be claimable on an undated or stopped cheque, or one which the drawer was fraudulently induced to issue.

A bearer cheque is negotiated by handing over – if payable to order it must be endorsed by signing it, the signatory thereby becoming liable for the amount – *and* delivering it to another holder. If no endorsee is named, any name can be written above an endorsing signature. If you are signing or endorsing on behalf of someone else, limit or negative personal liability by signing 'for and on behalf of' your principal or the business *and* describing the capacity in which you sign. Company names must be on all negotiable instruments, endorsements and orders for money and directors endorsing as guarantors are liable to both drawer and holder. One signatory can stop payment on joint company or partnership accounts but one partner's signature is normally sufficient on cheques paid by, or to, the business. Cheques made out to more than one payee must be endorsed by them all, unless one has authority to sign for the others. You can direct endorsees to be paid jointly on the cheque but the face value cannot thereafter be split.

Lending money on an accommodation cheque – by post-dating it and making it payable to someone who makes a loan to a third party – makes you liable to a holder for value.

Banker's drafts

A draft is an order for payment made by the payer's bank and the bank is the drawer and drawee. The amount, place of payment and the name of the beneficiary/payee appear on the draft which when crossed works like a cheque.

Promissory notes

Promissory notes are conditional or unconditional promises to pay on demand, or on a fixed or determinable future date, a fixed sum to, or to the order of, a specified person or to bearer. They can be made payable with interest or in instalments and can provide that if an instalment is unpaid, the full amount becomes due.

A note need only be presented for payment if a place is specified and endorsers are only liable if it has been presented. With some exceptions a note-holder's legal rights and remedies are the same as those of a holder of a bill of exchange.

Bills of exchange

A bill is an unconditional order in writing addressed by one person (the drawer) to another (the drawee), signed by the drawer, requiring the drawee (who, when he or she signs, becomes the acceptor) to pay on demand or at a fixed or determinable future date, a fixed sum to, or to the order of, a specified person or bearer (the payee). Bills are more easily negotiated than cheques and notes; the right to future payment can be more flexible and is more saleable for immediate cash.

The differences between bills and cheques are as follows:

■ Bills can be drawn on anyone, a cheque only on a bank.
■ Bills can be payable on demand or in the future – cheques only on demand.
■ Bills must be presented for payment, or the drawer and endorser are discharged; a cheque drawer is liable for six years.
■ Cheques can be crossed, bills cannot.
■ Paying and collecting banks are more exposed when dealing with bills than cheques.
■ Unless payable on demand, bills are usually 'accepted'. A cheque is not usually accepted, so the drawer is primarily liable.
■ A bill, but only rarely a cheque, can be 'backed' – ie endorsed by someone who is neither drawer nor acceptor and who is liable to a holder in due course. It is backed when sold at a discount for immediate payment, the extra credit cover increasing the discount value.

A bill can be an order to pay from a fund or account, or set out the transaction giving rise to the debt. The value given for payment does not appear on the bill and where it is drawn or payable need not be stated.

A bill can be payable on demand, at sight, on presentation, at a determinable future date, after a fixed period after date or sight, after a fixed period after a specified event *but not on a contingency*. If no time is specified, it is payable on demand.

Interest or payment by instalments can be included with a provision that if an instalment is unpaid the full amount becomes due. If payable in foreign currency the rate of exchange can be specified, otherwise it is calculated according to the rate for sight drafts at the place of payment on the due date.

Bills drawn and payable within the UK or drawn or accepted on a UK resident are inland bills; other bills are foreign. The main difference is that foreign bills must be 'protested' if dishonoured, otherwise protesting may be optional. And inland bills are usually 'sola' ie drawn up in one part. Foreign bills can be drawn in sets of two or three parts (copies), each referring to the others, to protect against loss. You should accept and endorse only one.

Bills must be presented for acceptance and payment on the due date. Strictly, this is only necessary if payable after sight (when acceptance fixes maturity date), if specifically required, or if payable anywhere except the drawee's business or residential address. But they should be presented to secure the drawee's liability and the bills can then be negotiated and discounted – if the drawee refuses acceptance, the holder can immediately turn to the drawer. If the drawee later accepts it, acceptance is backdated to the date on which the bill was first presented for payment.

Bills can be accepted before the drawer signs or when overdue after dishonour except for bills payable after sight which are dishonoured if not accepted. Acceptance can be:

■ general – unconditional affirming the drawer's order; or
■ qualified – conditional and can be of a partial amount only. The holder can refuse this – unless it is partial acceptance of face value – and treat the bill as dishonoured. Drawer and endorsers are then discharged from liability. Partial acceptance can only be protested as to the balance.

Bills must be presented for payment and acceptance before overdue unless payable on demand, when they can be presented for payment any time. Presentment is usually at the acceptor's or drawer's address and, if agreed, can be by post. All joint acceptors or drawers must be presented with it, unless one has authority to accept for them all. If an acceptor or drawer is bankrupt or dead, the bill can be treated as dishonoured or can be accepted by the trustee in bankruptcy or personal representatives but must first be presented. Although drawer and endorsers are usually discharged from liability if a bill is not presented for payment on the due date, the acceptor remains liable unless he has stipulated it must be presented for payment. If not accepted within a reasonable time, notice of dishonour can be given to drawer and endorsers but if the bill is not 'noted' or 'protested' the right of recourse against them may be lost.

Drawer and endorsers are liable when bills are dishonoured on present-ment for payment. Non-payment of accepted bills gives a right of immediate action against the drawer as acceptor without having to protest the bill or give notice of dishonour.

Generally, notice of dishonour must be given to all parties, in writing or in person, on the day of dishonour or the next working day. Foreign bills require proof of presentation and dishonour. The bill must be re-presented by a notary public and refusal of acceptance or payment is 'noted' on the bill – a declaration (the 'protest') is then made in a separate document. Although not required for inland bills it is safest to do both.

Overseas payments

Overseas business is usually done under letters of credit or documentary or acceptance credits issued by banks or accepting houses, who lend their name where a buyer or seller is unknown or there is doubt about the economic and/or political situation. Interest rates vary with the risk and the trader's credit-standing.

For importers some banks require partial cash cover. The bank issues a letter of credit in favour of the supplier, undertaking to accept his or her bill drawn on them if accompanied by shipping documents. The supplier's bank buys the bill for cash and sends it with the shipping documents for presentation and acceptance to the importer's bank who releases the documents to the importer, so that he or she can take delivery.

Overseas customers can open irrevocable documentary acceptance credits in their favour at their foreign bank. Their London branch takes the bills for current shipments on the security of the shipping documents. When accepted they can be discounted.

Importers can also arrange acceptance credits with acceptance houses or banks who accept bills drawn on them subject to conditions, but again they may require partial cash cover. The proceeds then go to the bank's overseas agents who pay the supplier when he or she hands over the shipping documents. Alternatively, an overseas supplier may arrange with a London bank to draw bills on the security of the shipping documents, which are released to you against payment. They may have a documentary credit with a London bank to negotiate bills drawn by you on them. The bills are presented to the London branch which sends them to the overseas customer's bank where they are surrendered for cash or against acceptance of the bills.

Overseas suppliers can also draw sight or time bills on UK customers. Sight bills are sent to the UK with the shipping documents and presented to the importer for payment against delivery of the documents. With time bills the importer arranges a credit with a foreign branch or correspondent of his or her bank who buys it at the bank's buying rate of exchange for similar UK drafts. The importer accepts it on D/A terms (documents against acceptance) when the goods are delivered on arrival or are warehoused and insured at the importer's expense until the bill is paid at maturity, although he or she may be able to take earlier delivery by paying a premium.

Acceptance credits are often made on a revolving basis: when drafts mature, new drafts are drawn up to an agreed maximum. Raw materials are sometimes bought through London acceptance houses by acceptance credit. Drafts are accepted up to a specified amount drawn on the bank by a manufacturer, usually payable three months after date. The manufacturer must put the bank in funds at or before maturity date by way of cash or bills which can be discounted when accepted.

The Export Credits Guarantee Department (ECGD) offers credit insurance by way of guarantees direct to exporters and on goods and services sold on credit terms to the financing bank.

Different arrangements apply to ECGD support for UK exports to the EU and unconditional guarantees are available.

Cover on loans through foreign banks can also be arranged through the ECGD. Information and advice is available from your own bank and the government services, including the DTI.

Information about insurance for importers on credit purchases is obtainable through the Department for Trade and Industry. Similar schemes to the ECGD's are available if you are buying abroad and buyer credit guarantees from the supplying country may be available.

Selling debts

You can sell debts for cash under a factoring agreement, which sets out your undertakings as to the status of the debts, the factor's rights and the price paid for advance payment. The factor acts as a collection agent and is responsible for keeping accounts. You usually receive immediate payment of up to 80 per cent of the invoices accepted and the balance when the debt is paid, less the factor's charges, usually a percentage of turnover. The initial lump sum payment will also be discounted at a rate similar to bank charges on secured overdrafts, plus a flat monthly fee or a percentage of turnover. The agreement may attract stamp duty and should be registered as an assignment of book debts under the Bills of Sale Act or the Companies Act. Some banks offer a factoring service, buying debts at a discount on the security of invoices and interest is charged on the payment at a rate that is usually about the same as bank interest charged on secured overdraft facilities. You receive the balance of the face value of the invoice when the debt is paid. Other variations are *non-recourse factoring*, which provides 100 per cent credit cover on approved debts and *recourse factoring*, which usually provides more cash but no credit protection.

With invoice discounting, you retain control of the sales ledger and chase debts yourself. Again, you receive up to 80 per cent of accepted invoices and the balance less the discounter's charges when the debts are paid and, again, the charge is a discount on the initial lump sum payment plus a flat monthly fee or a percentage of turnover.

Statutory references

Banking Act 1979
Bank of England (Time of Noting) Act 1917
Bills of Exchange Act 1882
Cheques Act 1957 and 1992
Companies Act 1985
Consumer Credit Acts 1974 and 2006
European Communities Act 1972
Limited Liability Partnership Act 2000

11

Patents, copyright and trademarks

Goods, services and anything manufactured, marketed or produced which depend for profitability and/or marketability on novelty or brand name is 'intellectual property'. Like any other property, the law protects it.

Protection provided by the law

Protection varies but is principally aimed at stopping competitors exploiting your product or process without consent and covers:

- patent law – protecting 'uniqueness' of technological inventions;
- copyright – protecting literary, artistic and musical works, computer programs and databases, films, recordings, broadcasts and cable programmes;
- design right – protecting the appearance of mass-produced articles;
- trademarks – protecting commercial labels;
- protection against competitors disparaging your products maliciously and 'passing off' their products as yours;
- commercial exploitation of industrial secrets.

"Can you access copyright publications in an instant? **We can**."

Do you photocopy or scan extracts from magazines, books or journals?

If so we can help. CLA advises small businesses how to gain access to articles and extracts from copyright publications easily and legally.

And to make life simpler, we offer 'blanket coverage' licences so you don't have to contact individual publishers each time you make a copy.

The CLA also represents and protects the interests of authors, artists and publishers to ensure they get fairly rewarded for the use of their intellectual property.

The cost of an annual small business licence starts from as little as £103.

To find out more about how copyright affects your organisation, or to apply for a licence, simply call us on 0800 085 6644 or visit www.cla.co.uk

Protecting the value of creativity

The **Copyright**
Licensing Agency

Rights are enforced by similar actions in the civil courts but costs vary. Patent actions are the most lengthy, complicated and costly and often cease to be commercially important before trial. The award or decision is binding. The Department for Constitutional Affairs (DCA) actively promotes Alternative Dispute Resolution (ADR) and litigating parties may be punished in costs if they refuse to mediate.

Copyright, trademark and passing off actions can be brought to trial within months and cost far less. Actions for infringing industrial design vary in cost and complexity, depending on the conduct of the action and the approach.

An interlocutory – pre-trial – injunction ordering a defendant not to continue or to embark on a course of action until trial is a fast and relatively cheap route but the plaintiff must in return undertake to compensate the defendant if the case is lost. If the plaintiff then wins, he or she can obtain a continuing injunction, delivery up or destruction of infringing items and compensation for financial loss. Trademark owners may also claim advertising costs for restoring their position, copyright and patent owners can claim compensation for forced reductions in price pending trial, and plaintiffs in passing off and slander of goods actions can claim compensation for damage to goodwill. Copyright owners can also claim damages for conversion, ie for work sold, or destroyed by, or as a result of, infringement. There may also be criminal liability and an offence under the Trade Descriptions Acts, bringing fines and penalties, including imprisonment and forfeiture or destruction of the offending goods and materials.

It is proposed to introduce voluntary Alternative Dispute Resolution (ADR) in the Patents County Courts to provide low cost handling of intellectual property disputes to be heard by specialist single arbitrators whose award or decision will be binding. Mediation is part of the package which should offer a fast and relatively cheap route to a legally enforceable settlement.

Patents

Patent law gives temporary protection to unique articles and manufacturing processes superior to their predecessors and a properly drawn up patent gives a complete monopoly. Novelty is the basis of a patent and the product's importance decides whether competitors risk legal action or try to avoid your monopoly. The length of the protection may be decisive as to the practicability of competitors doing the necessary work to sidestep your patent.

Patent litigation is expensive but disputing parties can choose instead to ask the Patent Office for an opinion on patent validity and infringement.

Patent protection abroad is obtained through national applications in each country or under the European Patent Convention (EPC). A single EPC application through the London Patent Office (www.patent.gov.uk) or the EU Patent Office in Munich (www.european-patent-office.org) grants a bundle of national patents. Enforcement and validity are determined by national law so results may not be consistent. The Convention is not an European Community Treaty but a treaty between contracting parties.

Most but not all of the EU is covered and eventually there will be a single patent enforceable throughout the EU. If you are resident or domiciled in the UK and have clearance from the UK Patent Office you can register patents in any of the signatory states named in your application to the London or European Patent Office.

Agreements restricting competition

The following agreements should be drafted by specialists to ensure compliance with both British and EU law.

Patent licences

The manufacture, import, sale and use of patented articles or processes is only lawful with the consent of the patent holder, and with important exceptions you can agree any terms. When you license manufacture, it is implied you can use and sell the product/process yourself. Anyone knowing of restrictions must comply with them or risk infringement but not every restriction is lawful. Under EU law you cannot limit inter-product competition which precludes granting an exclusive licence but there are some block exemptions. British law is also restrictive and you cannot usually force a licensee to buy unpatented materials, although you can agree preferential terms on unpatented goods if you comply with EU law.

Know-how licensing

These also restrict competition in breach of both British and EU law but there are individual and block exemptions.

Research and development

Cooperation agreements for research and development are usually permitted under EU law and, although conditions are strictly defined, some agreements are specifically exempt.

Copyright

Copyright, design right, computer programs and e-commerce are protected under copyright law. E-commerce covers electronic transmission, digital broadcasting and 'on-demand' services; copy protection systems and digital watermarks are also protected. The European Copyright Directive, amending the Patents Act 1977, brings our patent system into line with the European Patent Convention and strengthens the enforcement of patent rights and the resolution of disputes. The amendments also restrict the type and scope of permitted exceptions to copyright and:

- Grant performers exclusive right to control 'on-demand' transmissions of recordings of performances.
- Permit some exceptions to reproduction right for some temporary, transient or incidental acts.
- Grant increased protection to technological measures used by right holders, other than computer programmers, against unauthorised reproduction and copyright infringements.
- Enable right holders of electronic right management information (RMI) to identify, track and assist with utilisation of works, including the conditions applying for the acts to be considered unlawful. The RMI must be associated with the copyright work. (This is entirely new in our copyright law.)

And there are increased sanctions and remedies.

AT BECK GREENER we do much more than simply protect new ideas. Our comprehensive professional service and in depth experience enable us to guide you from initial concepts to commercial success.

Intellectual property protection is of paramount importance to any business. We provide expert advice based on a wealth of experience in the field. We always aim to give the best professional service whether we are dealing with the individual inventor or a major multinational.

We protect inventions from simple mechanical toys to complex new drug formulations requiring global protection. We protect famous brands worldwide, and we help start-ups

New ideas need expert protection if you want them to soar

to identify and protect a name or logo with the potential to become a famous brand of the future.

The UK's role in Europe continues to develop and the European aspect of our work becomes ever more important. All our patent partners are experienced European patent attorneys and represent clients directly before the European Patent Office.

Similarly, we act directly at the Office for Harmonization of the Internal Market (OHIM) obtaining and defending Community trade marks and designs.

If you require professional services in the field of intellectual property, we can help. Please contact one of our partners: For trademark matters contact Ian Bartlett. For patent matters contact Jacqueline Needle.

Patently an Investment
Jacqueline Needle, Beck Greener

When Ron Hickman was making his work bench in his garage, and selling it by mail order, he might have thought it too expensive to patent his invention. Fortunately, he did not, and Black & Decker had to pay him licence fees to make and market their famous "Workmate". The patents also enabled Hickman to stop competitors from making and selling their own versions of what has remained a very profitable product.

There are many more examples of innovative products making individuals and companies wealthy not only because of the inherent merits of the products, but also because they were appropriately protected by Intellectual Property Rights (IP).

James Dyson founded a company, which, because of his successful use of the patent system, was enabled to manufacture and sell vacuum cleaners particularly profitably, and in the process he became a millionaire. Dyson licensed his patents to companies in other countries, most notably to a company in Japan, such that the worldwide manufacturing capacity for his cleaners was enhanced. Dyson was also able to keep versions of the vacuum cleaner made by competitors, most notably by Hoover, off the market.

Unfortunately, those who run small businesses in the UK and Europe generally believe that IP rights, and patents in particular, are:
- irrelevant to small and growing businesses,
- difficult, if not impossible, to enforce, and
- expensive.

A research project in 2000 amongst companies in Europe established that only 30% of smaller companies in the UK, France, Germany, Italy, Spain, the Netherlands, Sweden and Finland had ever applied for a patent.

IP is difficult and expensive?
Individuals and companies can succeed and make money without involving themselves in IP issues. However, such an approach is not risk or expense free. There are many examples of companies who have ignored IP completely only to be

accused of patent or trademark infringement. The champagne at a product launch party can taste very flat if it arrives with an unexpected court injunction requiring that sales of the product cease. The expense of dealing with such accusations will be significant. Even worse, this unexpected expense could have been avoided.

IP does cost money, and if the issues are not understood, it can appear difficult. However, without IP, creativity cannot be captured and protected and it is this protection which enables ideas to be turned into wealth. The difficulties disappear with knowledge and SMEs ought to ensure that there is at least one person in authority who has been educated in IP.

Not all IP rights cost money. Copyright and unregistered design rights arise automatically. A company needs to keep the original software or design documents in a systematic way so that the date of origination can be established, and the creator or author identified. The company also needs to ensure that it owns the rights it uses in its day to day business. For example, a company commissioning a logo design will not automatically own the copyright in the resulting logo. A specific agreement will be required to transfer the copyright from the designer to the company.

Patent Office records can be freely searched on the internet for information about the trade marks which have been registered. A company can avoid conflict problems by ensuring that their chosen trade mark or logo is not already registered by someone else.

It does cost money to pay professional patent attorneys to register trade marks and to draft and file patent applications, but the potential rewards are high. For the price of one full page advert in the "Daily Telegraph" it would be possible to cover the costs arising over a five year period to obtain grant of a patent for a new invention in a selection of five European countries, in the USA, and in Japan. The newspaper may be in the bin within 24 hours, whilst the patents could provide a platform for profitable trading for 20 years.

Irrelevant for SMEs?
All businesses, regardless of their size, have competitors, and seek commercial advantages over those competitors. A small company coming into conflict with the rights of others does not have the commercial "muscle" that large

corporations can use to force a settlement. IP rights might be the only weapons an SME can deploy in the event of a conflict. Effective use of IP could be vitally important to SMEs.

Any proprietary information of commercial value should be identified and kept confidential. Employees should be made aware that such confidential information must not be divulged, and departing employees should be reminded that their duty of confidentiality will remain even after they have left. Both the recipe for Coca-Cola and the exact composition of the batter for Kentucky Fried Chicken are still known to only a handful of people.

A majority of those made rich with the assistance of IP, such as James Dyson and Ron Hickman, have had ideas or inventions which have been patented. A patent can only help if it is valid, and a valid patent can only be obtained if the patent application is filed before there has been any public disclosure of the invention. It is essential that any new idea of potential worth is kept totally confidential to the company during the early stages of design or development.

It is important to get the patenting decision correct, especially if a project is thought to be of potential value to the company. Not only must an invention be new to be patentable, it must also be non-obvious compared to what is already known. However, many inventors will wrongly define the final result of their labours as obvious. Similarly, the inexperienced are often heard to exclaim incorrectly, but with certainty: "you can't patent that".

If the invention has taken time and money to develop, will take further resources to get into the market, and is forecast to have a future, there is a very high chance that the invention will be patentable. In such circumstamces it would be wise to take professional advice.

IP rights are difficult to enforce?

It is commonly said that patenting an invention is a waste of time because the company will not be able to afford to enforce the patent. However, less than 1% of all patents are involved in any dispute, and it is the existence of the patent, rather than of the invention, which provides the wealth generating opportunities.

If a product newly on the market is successful it will soon attract the attention of competitors. They will want to provide their own versions and thereby share in the potential profits. If the product is not patented, the competitors are free to use the idea, although they cannot make a slavish copy. Domestic, electrically powered, air fresheners were put on the UK market one September some years ago as the "new, ideal Christmas gift". By October there were in excess of ten competing devices available such that the originator's Christmas market was literally decimated.

If the new product is patented, or is the subject of a patent application, the majority of businesses will pause before rushing to develop rival versions. Even large business is reluctant to get involved in patent litigation without good commercial reasons. When Xerox introduced the first generation of copying machines, they had a worldwide monopoly for the 20 years for which their patents existed without having to take action for patent infringement.

The competition is attracted by success, and so infringement actions are generally about inventions which make money. This profit stream alone might be enough to enable a patent action to be funded. It is also possible to take out legal expenses insurance to fund such actions.

The professionals who act for business in protecting their ideas and innovations, who ensure that their clients do not come into conflict with the rights of others, and who can advise when things go wrong, are Chartered Patent Attorneys (CPAs). Most UK CPAs are also European Patent Attorneys and not only obtain European patents, but also apply for and obtain Community designs and Community trade marks.

Jacqueline Needle is one of the select group of patent attorneys in the United Kingdom with a Litigator's Certificate which gives her the right to conduct litigation in IP matters in all of the English courts. Jacqueline has extensive experience of patent drafting and prosecution both in the United Kingdom and in other countries. She is a partner of Beck Greener in London and can be contacted at:
jneedle@beckgreener.com Tel: 020 7693 5600
The Beck Greener website: www.beckgreener.com

Additional royalties are payable for some uses of copyright material, eg photocopying books and journals by businesses that no longer falls within the scope of the fair dealing exception permitting fair dealing (see page 186). You should check with the Copyright Licensing Agency to see if you are covered by an existing industry licence for larger-scale business photocopying.

At the time of writing it is unclear what effect this provision has on the licensing arrangements for royalties on sound recordings.

The Copyright Licensing Agency website on www.cla.co.uk has information about licences and guidance about changes in copyright law. Downloading or copying some online material, even for personal use, is a criminal offence, and any kind of technology that enables someone to play your legitimately acquired and copyright-protected CDs or DVDs on their PC is illegal.

Most industrial designs are copyright through initial drawings or prototype models, and copyright exists as soon as pen is put to paper or the model takes shape without registration or legal formalities. There is no copyright in an idea and others with the same idea have their own copyright but your copyright stops exact copying.

Copyright gives the owner the right to stop others from doing something.

If recorded in writing (ie in notation or code, by hand or otherwise) copyright covers:

- original literary, dramatic works (including dance or mime) – no aesthetic merit or style is required, so lists, catalogues, etc are included;
- computer programs, databases and software products;
- original musical works – ie music excluding words or action;
- part or all the typographical arrangements of published editions of literary, dramatic and musical works;
- original artistic works comprising graphics (photographs, sculptures or collages irrespective of artistic quality), architecture (buildings or models for buildings) and works of artistic craftsmanship;
- original sound recordings, films, broadcasts, teletext, satellite and cable programmes.

The 'author' is usually the first owner. Otherwise the first owner is:

■ the creator of literary, dramatic, musical and artistic works;
■ the person responsible for undertaking arrangements for making computer programs;
■ the person undertaking arrangements for making original sound recordings, films and cable programmes;
■ the person making broadcasts;
■ the employer for work done in the course of employment but the creator may retain moral rights *and* the publisher is the owner of published works.

Both 'author' and country of first publication must qualify for protection. Broadly, protection covers British citizens, subjects and nationals, citizens of British dependent territories, British protected persons domiciled or resident in the UK and in countries covered by the Act and companies incorporated under British law for 70 years. For design right protection, qualifying countries extend to cover member states of the EU.

'Premier league' electronic and paper database creators are protected for the life of the 'author' plus 70 years whether or not the database is innovative. For 'first league' databases the period is life plus 15 years. 'Premier league' databases, eg *Yellow Pages*, indicate by their complex structure that some 'intellectual creativity' was involved, while 'first league' databases, eg telephone directories, are compiled through a basic mechanical arrangement of information. But the dividing line is unclear. Records of how a database was created using intellectual effort could help in obtaining maximum protection and unless created by employees, you should require creators to assign copyright to you or the business.

These apply to all and a substantial part of the works and there is infringement if any of the following are done without the owner's consent:

■ copying, ie making a facsimile copy, including reduction or enlargement;
■ issuing copies to the public, including renting out sound recordings, films and computer programs – but only when first issued;

- publicly performing literary and dramatic works, including audio and visual representations and publicly playing and showing recordings, films, broadcasts and cable programmes;
- broadcasting or including the work in cable service;
- adapting and translating literary, dramatic and musical works, and doing any of the above in relation to an adaptation.

Permitted acts include:

- 'Fair dealing' with a substantial part of a work – this allows use compatible with fair practice and justified in the circumstances, eg for criticism and reporting, *but* copying of literary, dramatic, musical and artistic works is only permitted for private study, research or educational purposes *and* reprographic copying and a fee is payable to the author if the copying is done for commercial purposes. Copying some public documents is restricted.
- Performing, playing and showing works for educational purposes.
- Copying works in electronic form if purchased on terms that permit it.
- Rental of computer programs 70 years from the end of the year of first public issue.
- 'Reasonable extracts' of public readings in sound recordings, broadcasts or cable programmes unless expressly prohibited.
- Copying works other than broadcasts, cable programmes and typographical arrangements for use within 28 days by broadcasters and cable programme operators.

Not-for-profit and educational organisations do not need your consent to produce large print, braille and audio editions of your copyright works.

'Authors' of literary, dramatic, musical and artistic works and film directors have moral rights personal to them which cannot be assigned. Rights extend to adaptations and false attribution and essentially give rights to be given credit and have the creation respected. They cover:

- harm to reputation;
- 'paternity right' – to be identified (*but* not for computer programs or typeface design);

Protect what's rightfully yours

Patents and Trade Marks are among the most valuable tools for developing your new business.

At Brookes Batchellor, our Patent and Trade Mark Attorneys can arrange for the protection of your invention, brand name or design in the UK, EU or anywhere in the world.

We take a positive, comprehensive and creative approach to patent, trade mark and design law and put high quality service to our clients first. This is manifest in proven results and client satisfaction.

So, to protect what's rightfully yours, contact us on 020 7253 1563 or 01892 510600.

Brookes Batchellor

www.brookesbatchellor.co.uk

102-108 Clerkenwell Road, London EC1M 5SA. Tel 020 7253 1563 Fax 020 7253 1214
1 Boyne Park, Tunbridge Wells, Kent TN4 8EL. Tel: 01892 510600 Fax: 01892 510666

Email: post@brookesbatchellor.co.uk   Brookes Batchellor LLP is a Limited Liability Partnership

BROOKES BATCHELLOR LLP

How can we help you? Let's consider your new product –

Its construction:

Why should I apply for a patent? A valid patent will protect your investment in innovation. A patent may allow you to improve your negotiating position with customers, competitors, suppliers and sales agents as well as enabling you to enter markets presently beyond your reach via licences. In industries which cannot compete on manufacturing costs a patent may be an essential element in defending your business against competition. A patent may provide security to assist you in financing your business. Patents have been used to enhance the value of shares and to enhance a brand image in marketing.

Its name:

Why should I register my trade mark? It's not just the brand name you have devised that is a Trade Mark; a Trade Mark is any sign which is capable of distinguishing goods or services of one undertaking from those of other undertakings. A Trade Mark may consist of a word or words (including personal names), designs and logos, letters, numerals or the shape of goods, their packaging, smells and sounds. A Trade Mark is a property right and can be assigned, sold or licensed to other traders. The name of your product is an important factor in persuading the public to associate the product with your business. So a Trade Mark is a powerful marketing tool, and can become a valuable property right for a business.

Its appearance:

Why should I register my design? Registration of a design can protect the appearance of the whole or part of a product and in particular protect the features of shape, configuration, pattern and ornament-lines, contours, colours, shape, texture, materials or ornamentation of a new design. The appearance of your product is an important factor in persuading the public to associate the product with your business.

So come and talk to us:

Brookes Batchellor LLP is a firm of Patent and Trade Mark Attorneys, with main offices in London and Tunbridge Wells, and a satellite office in the Kent Science Park in Sittingbourne.

The present firm was formed in 2001 from the merger of two long established partnerships, Brookes & Martin and Batchellor Kirk & Co. The "Brookes" in our name can be traced back to 1852, as William Brookes was one of the first Patent Agencies in the UK.

However, as well as our history, we are a modern European and UK firm using the latest technologies and techniques to serve clients in a wide range of industries. We are committed to providing a personal service that operates consistently to the highest professional and technical standards, whether acting for multinational corporations, or for private individuals.

As UK and European Patent and Trade Mark Attorneys, we have broad experience in relation to all aspects of Intellectual Property, including patents, trade marks, design right and design registration, and copyright. We have expertise in patenting all technical fields including electronics, software, pharmaceuticals, chemistry, mechanical engineering and physics.

We routinely file and prosecute patent, trade mark and design registration applications within the UK and EU, internationally through the Patent Cooperation Treaty and Madrid Protocol, and on a worldwide basis in conjunction with a network of overseas attorneys. We conduct searches for earlier rights, and advise clients on the ownership, transfer and licensing, renewal and enforcement of their rights.

We can help you – to protect what is rightfully yours!

www.brookesbatchellor.co.uk

- ■ 'right of integrity' – to object to derogatory treatment, ie additions, alterations and adaptations other than translation or change of musical key or register if there is distortion or mutilation, or honour or reputation is prejudiced (*but* computer programs and reports of current events are excluded);
- ■ right to privacy of some photographs and films;
- ■ the right not to have the work changed and possibly to have it maintained in good condition;
- ■ exclusive right to authorise publication;
- ■ right to withdraw and revise the work.

An employer owning copyright has no moral rights and they do not apply to fair dealing and incidental inclusion in sound recordings, films, broadcasts or cable programmes.

Rights are infringed by possession, sale, hire, rental or exhibition in the course of business or distribution which affects the author or director's honour or reputation.

Rights can be assigned in writing but only exclusive licences must be in writing. You can assign future rights and assignments for part of the copyright period.

The owner and exclusive licensee can stop infringement by injunction and obtain:

- ■ search warrants and orders for delivery up and seizure of infringing copies – in some circumstances owners can seize copies themselves;
- ■ accounts of profits;
- ■ damages – *but* not if the infringer did not know or had no reason to believe copyright subsisted;
- ■ an order restraining 'derogatory' treatment of moral rights of an author or director.

Devices for copy protection (software preventing unauthorised copying or use) are protected if the infringer knows or has reason to believe they are used for making infringing copies. They may also be protected under unfair competition law.

Broadly, these cover 'dealing', including importing and exhibiting, when the defendant knows or has reason to believe the articles are infringing copies and the 'consent or connivance' of a company's officers brings liability on them as well as the company.

Offences punishable with a fine and/or imprisonment are:

■ playing or showing infringing works *but* not receiving infringing broadcasts or cable progammes unless intending to avoid payment;
■ making or possessing articles designed or adapted for copying, knowing or having reasonable cause to believe they will be used to make infringing copies for sale, hire or use in business;
■ gaining unauthorised access to a computer system;
■ carrying out unauthorised modifications to, or erasing, a computer program.

The criminal courts can order search and seizure of infringing copies and Customs and Excise will stop imports at the owner's request.

Performers' protection and performance rights

Rights last 70 years from the end of the calendar year of the performance. Infringement is by recording, live transmission and possessing, using, importing and dealing in illicit recordings. Performers and those with whom they have exclusive contracts can consent to breach of copyright – even though the performer is in breach of contract – or sue for infringement. The court can order search, seizure, delivery up and destruction of recordings, films and equipment adapted to produce them and it is a criminal offence to make, deal with or use illicit recordings. Defences are similar to those in other criminal copyright proceedings and penalties include fines and/or imprisonment.

Data protection

If you store data about living individuals who can be identified from your electronic or paper records, you must register with the Information

Commissioner under the 1998 Data Protection Act. Forms and information are available from the Office of the Data Protection Registrar and an annual licence costs £35. Failure to comply with the Act can lead to prosecution, refusal of registration or service of enforcement transfer prohibition, or deregistration notices.

If requested, you must give data subjects details of the information stored, including its sources, uses, why it is held and to whom it is disclosed. You can charge a fee for the service. You can be required to cease processing the data if it is causing or is likely to cause unwarranted and substantial damage to the data subject or anyone else, and the data subject can apply to court for compensation. If the data is incorrect or misleading, you can be required to rectify, block, erase or destroy it, and the data subject can refer to the Commissioner to assess whether you are contravening the Act.

Non-disclosure of some data is permitted, including management forecasts, management planning and information relating to national security, crime, taxation, health, education and social work.

Design right

'Design right' gives the following periods of protection to registered designs and artistic works:

■ original non-commonplace designs of an article's shape or configuration – 10 years from first marketing with a 15-year limit from creation;
■ registered designs – a maximum of 25 years;
■ articles designed as artistic works exploited industrially – 25 years;
■ artistic works not exploited industrially – 50 years.

There can be partial transmission of some rights and of part of the protected period. Assignments must be in writing and, unless otherwise agreed, registered design right includes design right.

music *influences* *your* business...

...and we all know the benefit playing it has on your staff and customers. But, did you know that no matter the type of business, if you play copyright music on your premises, you need a licence from the Performing Right Society?

PRS collects royalties on behalf of its members - the writers and publishers of the music you play.

The Performing Right Society

Call us now for your PRS Music Licence

0800 068 4828

www.prs.co.uk

Music can be used as a great tool to influence the perception of your business. It can be used to create desired atmospheres. It can affect customer purchasing choice and entice people to stay for longer, select goods quicker or inspire a purchase. It can also improve morale and performance, by uplifting moods and entertaining staff whilst they are working.

If you do play copyright music to customers, visitors or your staff, you will legally need the permission of the people who wrote it. In the UK, you get that permission from PRS in the form of a PRS Music Licence.

PRS is a not-for-profit membership organisation of 44,000 composers, songwriters and music publishers. PRS collects and distributes the royalties created when this music is performed in public. The royalties PRS pays to these members as a result of you buying a licence are really important in sustaining them; and that keeps them writing more music for you to use and benefit from in your business. Playing music not only keeps your staff and customers happy but by buying a PRS Music Licence you join us in creating a future for music.

However you use music and whatever type of business you have, if copyright music is performed a PRS Music Licence is required. The music can be performed by any means, be it CD, radio, TV, music on hold, or even live performances, to anyone including; staff, visitors, or customers.

It is the responsibility of the owner/proprietor of the business to obtain a PRS Music Licence if music is being performed. Call **0800 068 4828** for a quote and to obtain your PRS Music Licence or for further information visit **www.prs.co.uk**

Rights are slightly different from copyrights:

■ Primary right is an exclusive right to reproduce commercially. There is primary infringement when articles are copied 'exactly or substantially to' the design. 'Kits' – 'complete or substantially complete' sets of component parts which infringe when made up are included.
■ Importing, possessing for commercial purposes, or dealing commercially with an infringing article knowing or having reason to believe it is such is secondary infringement.

There is a limited defence too of innocence and if the design is copyright and copyright is not infringed, there is no infringement of design right.

During the last five years of protection there is a 'licence of right' to perform restricted acts.

Design right owners and exclusive licensees have the same remedies as copyright owners and the court can also order forfeiture, destruction or other disposal of infringing articles. Unlike copyright, design right is effective only in the UK.

Non-functional designs, ie shapes, configurations or ornaments with eye appeal, applied to articles by an industrial process are protected by registration. The test of infringement is the eye of a customer interested in design. Registration is expensive but worthwhile if the design is an almost inevitable development in its field. It is then infringed by anyone using it, even if created entirely without reference to the design. The author is the original owner but the commissioner and employer are owners of commissioned designs and designs made in the course of employment.

The owner has exclusive rights to make, import for sale, hire or use for the purposes of trade and to sell, hire, offer or expose for sale or hire articles for which the design is registered and to which it, or one not substantially different, has been applied. Infringement is doing any of these without consent and making anything, or enabling anything to be made, to which the design is applied. Rights last for 5 years, extendable by 5-year periods to a maximum of 25 years. There is a six months' grace period at the end of each period to permit late application and rights can be restored if registration lapses.

It is proposed to introduce a community design system including a registered element to be administered by the Office for the Harmonization of the Internal Market in Alicante.

Confidential information

Information, including trade and technological secrets, commercial records and marketing, professional and managerial procedures, can be protected by obtaining undertakings to keep it confidential. This is only possible with those who receive information directly or indirectly and the law is reluctant to impose obligations on ex-employees to stop them using their knowledge and skill.

Domain names

A domain name – your label on the internet – protects your business name from 'cybersquatters'. Check the availability of the name online at registration agents' or authorities' sites, such as www.netnames.co.uk or www. nominet.com. There is usually a small charge but you do not need to establish a website to register a domain name.

Trademarks and service marks

Trademarks are defined as signs capable of being represented graphically and which distinguish your goods or services. They can be words, names, designs, letters, numerals, the shape of goods or packaging, or distinctive sounds or smells, provided they can be graphically represented.

Service marks identify services and are registered and protected in the same way as trademarks.

Collective marks which distinguish goods and services of members of an association are also protected. A trademark search shows existing and pending registrations, but the search is technical and you are advised to use a trademark agent. Details can be found at www.itma.org.uk, www.cipa.org. uk or www.patent.gov.uk. The agent can also check for rights of reputation or 'passing off' rights (see below).

Registration is refused if the mark:

- is not distinctive;
- consists of signs or indications designating the goods' or services' characteristics, eg quality, quantity, purpose, geographical origin, *unless* the mark is distinctive through use;
- is already established in the trade or in use;
- is likely to be confused with existing marks – *but* the owner of an earlier mark can consent to registration. If the applicant shows 'honest concurrent use', *or* the registration procedure for an earlier mark was completed for five years prior to the date of publication, registration is allowed.

Registration is for 10 years, renewable for further 10-year periods.

When the mark is registered the owner can prevent the use of:

- an identical mark for identical and similar goods/services;
- a similar mark for similar or identical goods/services if there is a likelihood of confusion;
- an identical or similar mark for non-similar goods/services where the infringer would take unfair advantage of or damage the owner's established reputation.

The owner can require infringing articles to be handed over and claim damages and infringers may be fined or imprisoned.

If the mark is well known but unregistered, the owner can stop use of a similar or identical mark for similar or identical goods/services and require infringing articles to be handed over but cannot claim damages.

Applications are made in the member states and rights are enforceable against imports from outside the EU. Owners in an EU member state can, however, only stop imports of goods with the same mark from another member state if they were wrongfully marketed in the exporting state by the exporter or marketed without the owner's consent in the importing country and there must be no link between the two owners. The owner cannot stop marked goods sold in the EU from being resold, even if the marks in member states have different owners.

Swindell and Pearson are a firm of Chartered and European Patent and Trade Mark attorneys active across a wide range of intellectual property matters.

The firm was established in the 1870's by William Swindell and has grown steadily since to meet the needs and aspirations of their growing client base.

We act for a range of companies from multi-national companies through plc's, Ltd companies and individuals, including Universities and research organisations. Our clients are spread around the world with many in the UK, including those local to our offices across the Midlands.

The matters we handle for our clients, include :

- Protecting our client's intellectual property rights
- Advising in relation to third party's intellectual property rights
- Monitoring and challenging where appropriate third party's intellectual property rights
- Dealing with infringements of our client's intellectual property rights
- Handling matters when our clients are accused of intellectual property infringement
- Advising in relation to appropriate intellectual property protection strategies

In relation to new inventions, concepts and ideas, we can:

- Advise on available types of intellectual property protection

- Propose strategies for obtaining protection in required geographical areas
- Obtain appropriate protection
- Assist with seeking appropriate ways to market

For protecting the appearance or decoration applied to articles, we can:

- Advise on the automatic and obtainable types of protection
- Obtain appropriate protection where required
- Consider and advise on third party design rights

In relation to trade marks and brands, we can:

- Check the availability of proposed marks
- Seek protection for trade marks around the world
- Advise on strategies for protecting brands
- Watch third party's trade mark cases, and advise and oppose such cases when required
- Advise in relation to potential infringement of client's trade mark rights
- Advise relative to allegations of trade mark infringements from third parties

We seek to add value to your business by providing relevant commercial advice and assistance in relation to your intellectual property rights and those of your competitors.

Please do not hesitate to contact us via our website **www.patents.co.uk** or by calling Robert Sales on **01332 367051**

Alternatively you can register a Community Trade Mark (CTM) with the Community Trade Mark Office in Alicante, Spain. The mark must be distinctive and the name must not mislead, or be contrary to EU public policy, or already be in use within the EU.

Registration gives EU protection and the owner will be able to stop imitation or use of the mark for similar goods and services or exploitation of its commercial value, but infringement proceedings will be governed by national law. Rights are transferable and can be licensed. Registration is for 10 years, renewable for a further 10 years but the owner must put the CTM to genuine use in the EU during the first 5 years.

The EU mark will eventually link into the world intellectual property system with headquarters in Geneva through which protection can be obtained in about 30 countries. The mark is circulated but it is processed in accordance with national laws and the applicant receives national registrations. International registration of trademarks can also be effected in member states signatories to the Madrid Protocol, which now include the United States.

Certification trademarks

These show that the owner's goods have reached a certified standard. Certification requires compliance with standards and use approved by the Department of Trade and Industry, details of which are obtainable from the Patent Office. Owners are usually trade or similar organisations and often manufacturers are authorised to apply the mark under the owner's supervision. The mark is not registered and ownership can only be transferred with the consent of the DTI.

Passing off

Passing off covers everything from dishonest trading to near infringement of trademarks, but actions are often concerned with business names because registration of a name gives no right to exclusive use. Most actions involve applying a distinctive badge, sign, label or distinctive package or appearance to goods, thereby implying they are someone else's. The badge must be something used by another trader which deceives, misleads or confuses the customer. There must be a real likelihood of financial loss and it is irrelevant whether other traders or the general public are misled and whether the deception is a mistake, an accident or fraudulent. You are entitled to compensation and an order forbidding continuance of the deception, but full trials are rare because of the difficulty of proving deception.

Slander of goods

This is also called slander of title, trade libel and injurious falsehood and consists of injury to someone's business by making a false and derogatory statement to a third party for an indirect or dishonest motive. The statement must be false and actual, or a genuine risk of financial loss must be proved.

Restrictive trade practices

Producers and suppliers of goods and services must register agreements where at least two parties restrict their conduct in one or more of the ways listed in the Competition Act 1998. The Act is concerned with unfair competition, particularly with terms relating to:

■ prices and charges;
■ terms and conditions of supply;
■ quantities, descriptions and areas for the supply of goods and services;
■ to and by whom goods and services are supplied;
■ manufacturing processes.

For instance, it is unlawful – as being against the public interest – for manufacturers or suppliers exclusively to tie traders to one dealer for spares.

Patent, registered design and copyright licences are not registrable if the only restrictions concern the invention, the article for which the design is registered, or the copyright. But again, it must be registered if at least two parties accept restrictions.

Exchange of information agreements may be exempt if they relate to manufacturing processes. Trademark licences may be exempt if restrictions relate only to goods bearing the mark or to manufacturing processes. Once registered, agreements can only be modified through the Restrictive Trade Practices Court or the Director of Fair Trading. If they are not price-fixing agreements the Director can state they are 'non-notifiable' and will not refer them to the Restrictive Trade Practices Court. The Director also has a discretion to accept undertakings from monopoly traders involved in anti-competitive practices.

The system is to be replaced by a general prohibition on agreements and concerted practices which have or may have the object or effect of preventing, restricting or distorting competition. The wording is similar to provisions in EU law rendering such agreements illegal.

There is an unlimited fine and up to five years' imprisonment for anyone responsible for horizontal price fixing, limiting supply or production, market sharing and bid-rigging. Company directors and LLP designated members may also be disqualified from holding office for up to 15 years. 'Whistleblowers' who cooperate in the investigation can obtain immunity from prosecution.

The Office of Fair Trading supplies information about registrable agreements and anti-competitive practices and further information may be available from your trade association.

This is, however, a complicated area, and if your contracts are likely to be affected, you should take legal advice.

Statutory references

Broadcasting Acts 1980 and 1996
Competition Act 1980 & 1998
Computer Misuse Act 1990
Consumer Credit Act 1974
Copyright and Related Rights Regulations 2003
Copyright, Designs and Patents Act 1988
Copyright etc and Trademarks (Offences and Enforcement) Act 2002

Copyright (Visually Impaired Persons) Act 2002
Criminal Damage Act 1971
Data Protection Act 1988
Defamation Act 1952
Deregulation and Contracting Out Act 1994
Design Copyrights Act 1968
Enterprise Act 2002
European Communities Act 19972
Fair Trading Act 1973
Legal Deposit Libraries Act 2003
Patents Acts 1977 and 2004
Patents (Amendment) Act 1978
Patents, Designs and Marks Act 1986
Registered Designs Act 1949
Trade Descriptions Acts 1968 and 1972
Trade Marks Act 1994
Video Recordings Act 1984 and 1993

Main international copyright treaties

Berne Convention for the Protection of Literary and Artistic Works
Rome Convention (the International Convention for the Protection of
Performers, Producers of Phonograms and Broadcasting Organisations)
Universal Copyright Convention
The World Intellectual Property Organisation Copyright Treaty and Per-
formances and Phonograms Treaty cover copyright and related rights

Every product or service that we use in our daily lives is the result of a long chain of big or small innovations, such as changes in design or improvements that make a product look or function the way it does today.

The Patent Office is the official government body responsible for granting Intellectual Property (IP) rights in the United Kingdom (UK). These rights include:

- Patents
- Trade marks
- Copyright
- Designs

Patents

A patent is a pact between you and the state. The state grants you the right to prevent anyone from making, using, selling or importing your invention for up to 20 years. In return, all the secrets of your new technology are published by the Patent Office, for anyone to read, 18 months after your application is filed.

To be worthy of patent protection an invention must have a practical application, not be obvious when compared with existing products or processes, and it must be novel: that is, not previously known anywhere in the world before the filing date of your patent  application. This means that not even you can talk about your invention, or show it at trade fairs or to potential customers prior to filing a patent application. Any disclosures made before patent filing must be covered by a confidentiality agreement. Once your patent application is received by the Patent Office you are free to disclose your invention however you like. By law patent applications must clearly and completely describe inventions and all patent applications are published if they are to be granted.

The maximum patent lifetime is 20 years. Once the patent is granted it is kept in force by the payment of annual renewal fees, starting at £50 in the fifth year, but rising gradually to £400 in the twentieth year. If you choose to stop paying the annual renewal fees (e.g. because the technology is getting out-of-date) then your patent will lapse immediately and become free for anyone else to copy.

A United Kingdom patent only affords you exclusive rights within the UK. To stop someone making, using, selling or importing your invention abroad, you will need patents in those foreign markets.

Although it costs just £200 in total fees to get a UK patent application to grant, the patent system has other costs. Your patent attorney could cost several thousand pounds. And your foreign filing costs will involve the use of foreign attorneys, and the fees of other national patent offices, and translation costs. Expect to pay around £6,500 for a US patent, £10,400 for a Japanese patent, and around £32,000 for patent protection across Europe once all the translation costs are included.

Trade marks

Trade marks are signs which distinguish the goods and services of one trader from those of others. Thus, while the formulation of, say, a washing powder sold under a particular registered trade mark may change many times over the years, a trade mark ensures that only the company, or its licensees, may sell a washing powder under that sign. Trade marks therefore provide protection for the goodwill and reputation of a firm in its products and services.

Trade marks, often the single most valuable marketing tool a company will have (whatever its size), do not need to be registered. Providing that sufficient trading reputation and goodwill has been built up in a mark, a degree of protection is afforded by common law. Registration of the mark on the other hand gives an immediate right to stop someone using the same or similar mark on the same or similar goods and services, without the need to prove reputation or demonstrate confusion.

A trade mark is any sign which can distinguish the goods and services of one trader from those of another. A sign includes, for example, words, logos, pictures, or a combination of these.

Basically, a trade mark is a badge of origin, used so that customers can recognise the product of a particular trader. To be registrable your trade mark must be: distinctive for the goods or services which you are applying to register it for, and not deceptive, or contrary to law or morality, and not similar or identical to any earlier marks for the same or similar goods or services.

Your registration lasts ten years from the date of registration. We will write to you a few months before the renewal date, asking if you wish to renew your trade mark for a further ten years. It costs £200 for the first class, plus £50 for each additional class, to renew your mark.

A United Kingdom trade mark only affords you exclusive rights within the UK. To stop someone using or selling goods bearing your name, logo etc. abroad, you will need trade marks in those foreign markets.

There are three routes to secure protection overseas: a series of individual trade mark applications, filed in each country; an application to OHIM, the Office for Harmonisation in the Internal Market, for a European Community trade mark registration, to secure trade mark protection in all EU countries; or, an application to the World Intellectual Property Organisation (WIPO) in Geneva, in order to obtain trade mark registration in a number of countries across the world.

The fee for an application is £200. This includes one class of goods or services from the list of 45 availiable classes. For every other class you apply for, it costs a further £50 for each class.

Using ™ does not indicate that a trade mark is actually registered, only that it is being used in a trade mark sense. A business would be breaking the law (Section 95 of the Trade Marks Act 1994) if it used the registered symbol ® or the abbreviation "RTM" when a mark is not registered.

Even if a mark is Registered a business does not have to identify a trade mark as registered. A business can choose to use the ® symbol or the abbreviation "RTM" (for Registered Trade Mark) to show that a trade mark is registered, but this could mean that the mark is registered somewhere other than in the UK. The ® symbol usually goes after the trade mark, in a smaller type size than the mark itself, and in a raised (superscript) position, but none of this is compulsory.

Copyright

Copyright is essentially a private right. You, the copyright owner must decide how to exploit your copyright work and how to enforce your copyright. A copyright owner can decide whether or not there will be any use of the copyright work falling within the scope of the economic rights and, if so, whether he or she will use the copyright work and/or license one or more other people to use the work.

A copyright owner can also benefit from copyright by selling or agreeing a transfer of copyright to someone else.

Many of the options available to a copyright owner will involve contractual agreements which may be just as important as the rights provided by copyright law. The right contractual agreement can minimise the chances of a dispute over use of your copyright work.

Designs

What is it that prompts us to buy a particular mobile phone, car, or toaster, is it the technology, is it the price? What about the way it looks? Where the technology and price may be similar, the eye-appeal of the product will be crucial for the market success or failure, whatever its other attributes. If the design of your product is a crucial element it should be protected.

Automatic or unregistered rights are free to obtain for artistic works, but difficult to enforce in the Courts because you must prove that the work in question is covered by copyright, that you own it, and that the alleged infringer copied your work. A design registration proves that the appearance of the product is protected, that you own it, and it enables you to take action against anyone making, using or selling your design without permission, even if they had not ever seen or copied your design.

So, what happens if you do not register my rights? In the best case scenario – nothing. Your ideas are not copied by competitors and your profits and reputation remain intact. In the worst case scenario – your inventions, brands, designs etc. are copied by your competitors, you lose the opportunity and ability to profit from them and your reputation with your customers is damaged.

Further information

The Patent Office web site provides a wide range of information (**www.patent.gov.uk**). There are a number of other organisations who will also be able to offer you advice and these include The Institute of Trademark Attorneys (**www.itma.org.uk**) and the Chartered Institute of Patent Agents (**www.cipa.org.uk**).

The Patent Office

PATENTS DESIGNS COPYRIGHT
TRADE MARKS

For Innovation

Patents
for inventions
Protecting the function of new products and processes.

Designs
for appearance
Protecting the unique look of parts or whole articles.

Copyright
for creative works
Literary, musical and artistic works, films, broadcasting and software.

Trade marks
for brands
Protecting distinctive reputations vested in names or logos.

Phone: 08459 500 505 Minicom: 08459 222 250
Fax: 01633 813600 www.patent.gov.uk

dti

A DTI SERVICE

12

Debt collection and litigation

Delayed payment has a disastrous impact on cash flow and profits, especially if interest rates are high. Effective credit control backed up by efficient debt collection with a prompt resort to law can help.

Records

Your customer lists should record full names and addresses of the businesses and proprietors. Credit should be given personally to the proprietors of businesses using a trading name.

Terms and conditions of business

Terms and conditions, including interest on delayed payments, should be included in quotations, estimates, acknowledgements of orders, invoices and delivery notes. They can include a right to retain title to goods until payment, but the term should be professionally drawn. They should be legible and intelligible. If referred to court, you will have to show they have been understood, particularly if dealing with consumers. In dealing with businesses – but not consumers – a separate agreement confirming acceptance of your terms and conditions is useful.

Avoid the pain of business failure

Why prepare for the worst, when we could help you lighten the burden of debt – and save your business?

The Business Debt Advisor can offer you:

- Sensible advice on business issues
- Friendly professional advice on practical solutions
- Free Confidential Advice

You'll find we're informal, friendly and effective. Visit our website right now, or call us on **0800 0825 1825** advice@thebusinessdebtadvisor.co.uk.

Your initial consultation is **free**, so you've got nothing to lose – and you could save your business. Doesn't that sound like a bright idea?

CALL FREE **0800 0825 1825**

www.thebusinessdebtadvisor.co.uk

The Right advice The Right solution Right now

 the*business*debtadvisor

Company Introduction

The Business Debt Advisor (TBDA) team has provided advice and assistance to hundreds of small and medium sized businesses.

The experienced team is headed up by Bev Budsworth, a licensed Insolvency Practitioner with over 20 years experience in corporate recovery and insolvency.

Bev Budsworth comments:

Entrepreneurship is the cornerstone of a successful economy. According to the Small Business Service, in 2005 there were more than 4.3 million business enterprises in the UK, and 99.3% of these were classed as 'small' that is, with fewer than 50 employees.

However, it's a fact that the majority of all new businesses fail. Whilst poor planning and ineffective management can account for some of the failures, in other cases its external factors such as losing a big contract or the insolvency of a major customer that can lead a business into a downward spiral of debt.

TBDA can help you to identify where things might be going wrong with your business. Maybe the bills are piling up and you don't know who to pay and when, perhaps the bailiffs are threatening to visit, or you may just not have enough cash to meet all your financial obligations each month.

Whatever your debt problem we can offer you friendly professional advice and practical solutions.

Case study

A 46-year-old engineering company was saved when its creditors agreed to a Company Voluntary Arrangement (CVA) – a formal agreement that freezes interest and charges and prevents creditors taking action. Over a four and a half year period, preferential creditors were paid in full and the company was able to repay 57% of its unsecured debts, which stood at over £100,000! The balance of the debt was legally written off!

The Directors comment:

We had never heard of a CVA and had concluded that the only solution was cessation of trade and liquidation. TBDA talked us through all the possible solutions and we were quite simply amazed that creditors would accept less than payment in full.

The team at The Business Debt Advisor were extremely professional and we are delighted with the outcome especially as they kept their costs to a minimum.

If included in your terms and conditions, you can claim interest after the period and at the rate specified in the contract 30 days after the period has elapsed. You can also include a term entitling you to reasonable recovery costs.

The right to charge interest and recovery costs should be stated on all written communications, credit application forms, order confirmations, invoices and contracts.

If you have no interest provision in the contract you can claim (statutory) interest at 8 per cent above current bank base rate plus reasonable recovery costs from the moment goods are delivered or services are performed. There is no right to interest on advance payments, unless otherwise agreed. If the contract requires payment in full or by instalments before goods are delivered or services performed, statutory interest runs from the day following delivery or performance. The credit period ends on the last day of the month following the month in which the invoice is received if your payments are usually made at the end of the month following receipt of the invoice.

Debtors in default must be given notice that statutory interest is to be claimed plus recovery costs. It is best to give written notice, so that you have a record. It should state the amount owed, the total interest due and the rate at which it will continue to accrue and to whom, where and when it must be paid and whether by cheque, electronic transfer or other means.

'Small businesses' can turn to a 'representative body' – any organisation representing small business, eg your trade association – to object to grossly unfair contractual terms, which, for instance, remove the right to statutory interest.

The Better Payment Practice Campaign has details of the statutory interest provisions and an interest calculator at www.payontime.co.uk.

Internal procedures

Limits should be put on credit. Cheques should be backed by banker's cards and the number written on the back of the cheque by the payee. Most cards guarantee payment of £50 to £100 and the cheque must cover only one invoice up to the stated limit, otherwise the bank can refuse to honour the cheque. For a fee, your bank will expedite presentation of cheques to the payer's bank. Payment by credit card is a contract, with the card holder as the card company's agent – if the card company becomes insolvent, you cannot sue the card holder.

Weekly or monthly balances should be kept on running accounts, with a cut-off point for legal proceedings. Small amounts should be paid promptly on delivery, preferably by cash or cheque – even post-dated. Acceptance of part payment in 'full and final settlement' does not debar further demands or court proceedings for the balance unless the debtor has given fresh consideration – ie done something to his or her detriment not called for under your agreement – in return for your agreement to take no further action.

Your best cover is a personal guarantee from the debtor and, if the amount is substantial, a third party, but before allowing a substantial debt to accrue or suing a debtor, it is worthwhile carrying out checks through searches at:

- Companies House;
- The Land Charges and Land Registry;
- The High Court Registers of
  - Bills of Sale;
  - Bankruptcy Petitions and Orders;
  - Deeds and Arrangements;
  - The Register of County Court Judgements on www.registry-trust.org.uk;

  but registration is against an address, not an individual, so check the entries actually relate to your debtor;
- Hire Purchase information Limited on www.isfra.ie/data/cr_pub_files/hire%20purchasepdf.

When legal action is inevitable, letters of demand should be worded carefully, setting a time limit for payment. Before issuing proceedings, you should deliver a standard 'letter before (legal) action' on which you can take proceedings.

Settling disputes by arbitration

It is worth considering arbitration. It can be flexible, fast and relatively cheap, specifically tailored to fit the dispute and heard by a specialist in the trade. Many trade organisations offer schemes, although some are thought to be biased in favour of their members. Consumers have the right to refer instead to the court, but the commercial court encourages litigants to consider the simpler and faster Alternative Dispute Resolution (ADR) and will, if appropriate, adjourn court proceedings while this is done.

Other forms of ADR include:

■ mediation, where a neutral trained mediator, who may be a lawyer, supervises without prejudice meetings leading to a legally binding agreement;
■ conciliation – here the conciliator intervenes, suggesting possible solutions;
■ med-arb, when mediation fails and the dispute is referred to arbitration, often before the mediator;
■ arbitration conducted by an agreed independent third party, a lawyer or appropriate expert, whose 'award'(decision) is legally binding and enforceable through the courts.

It is also worth considering early neutral evaluation conducted by a professional, usually a lawyer, who hears a summary of the case and gives a non-binding decision on the merits; or neutral fact-finding, which is more suitable for technical disputes when an agreed neutral expert looks at the facts and gives an evaluation on the merits.

Civil litigation

Litigation is a last resort, to be taken only if you expect to obtain payment and/or compensation. Commercial litigation is dealt with by the civil courts – the High Court and the County Court. The courts have similar procedure and debt collection is relatively straightforward. Experienced legal practitioners are best equipped to deal with the finer points of High

Court pleading and advocacy, and whatever the claim, you may face expensive opposition.

Sole traders, partners and directors with annual gross disposable income of up to £8,000 are eligible for legal aid, but not companies, and litigation is expensive. Leading firms charge hourly rates of £750-plus, but unless you have a specialist and substantial claim, you are unlikely to need the constant attention of the most senior partner or a QC. However, even in a fairly straightforward County Court claim, the bill can be several thousand pounds and, win or lose, you pay for work done before litigation.

The Gaming Act forbids some types of betting, but solicitors can now gamble on litigation and you may be able to proceed through conditional fee agreement. Your lawyers are entitled to a percentage of any winnings and insurance is available, but ensure all the terms of the contingency fee agreement are clearly spelt out. Alternatively, you may be able to obtain insurance cover for the litigation. Your solicitor will be able to give you details.

Your solicitor needs the facts, the documents (including a statement of account), relevant correspondence and details of a possible defence. If you are continuously referring debts to your solicitor, it is worth agreeing a standard referral procedure, with periodic summaries and settlement.

You can, however, litigate in person in any court and the small claims fast-track procedure in the County Court is specifically designed with this in mind. The emphasis here is therefore on suing in the County Court. If facts are in dispute or the claim is substantial, your best course is to instruct a solicitor.

Criminal proceedings

Crime is the business of the Magistrates' and Crown Courts and the police or responsible authority. It is no crime if debts are not paid or you carry on business at a loss unless fraud is involved. But you can be prosecuted under health and safety consumer protection, licensing, and road traffic legislation.

If you are prosecuted, whatever the circumstances, you need legal advice. Legal Aid is available but the decision to grant is for the court. The decision is based on a means test, whether the court would impose a custodial sentence and whether a conviction would lead to loss of livelihood or serious damage to reputation. Conviction can have serious repercussions in civil proceedings for compensation – conviction for a minor traffic offence linked to injury or property damage is automatically admissible, and negligence thereby proved in civil proceedings.

A prosecution in the Magistrates' Court is based on information stating that someone has, or is suspected of having, committed an offence. A summons or warrant to arrest is issued requiring the accused to appear in court. Warrants can only be obtained in specific circumstances, including for offences punishable with imprisonment and/or triable by jury.

More serious offences are heard in the Crown Court before a jury. The Crown Court also hears appeals from some civil decisions made in the Magistrates' Courts, eg decisions concerning licensing and recovery of unpaid income tax and NICs.

In police and in private prosecutions, an innocent party's costs may be paid if the accused is clearly innocent. But, as in any other litigation (unless there is full legal aid), innocent defendants pay part of the costs.

Civil actions

The High Court and the County Court deal with contractual, property and partnership disputes, business tenancies and tort claims. Contractual claims cover disputes about written or unwritten agreements. Claims in tort include claims in negligence, eg for compensation for injury or property damage caused in an accident. Straightforward cases are usually dealt with in the County Court. The High Court deals with more challenging cases and claims involving more substantial damages, professional negligence, fatal accidents, allegations of fraud or undue influence, defamation, malicious prosecution or false imprisonment and claims against the police.

County Court addresses are listed on www.hmcourts-service.gov.uk and information about procedure on www.direct.gov.uk. The County Court office will help you deal with forms and issue proceedings. District judges are used in cases involving up to £5,000. More important or complex cases and cases involving more than £5,000 are heard by a circuit or High Court judge.

Court fees are additional to your legal costs. You pay £30 to start an action claiming up to £300. The fee increases to a maximum of £1,700 for unlimited claims and claims for more than £300,000. Debt proceedings can be issued on line on www.moneyclaims.gov.uk. Fees start at £20 and payments are made by debit or credit card.

A defendant putting in a counterclaim – a money claim exceeding yours – pays the same fee and on the same basis as the claimant.

There is a fee of up to £500 for setting the case down for trial. You pay £35 when you apply for judgment, but only if the claim is defended.

The judge is the case manager and management includes pre-action protocols. These aim to encourage cooperation between the parties at an early stage in an effort to narrow the issues and, if possible, to avoid taking the case to trial.

The court is required to encourage and facilitate the use of alternative dispute resolution and can stay proceedings to allow for this either at the parties' request or when it considers this appropriate.

Cases are allocated to one of three tracks, depending on the complexity and amount involved, and the judge must:

- encourage the parties to cooperate;
- identify the issues at an early stage;
- dispose of summary issues that do not require full investigation;
- help the parties to settle all or part of the case;
- fix timetables for the hearing and control the progress of the case;
- consider whether the benefit of a particular method of hearing justifies its cost.

Parties refusing to comply may have their case struck out or face sanctions, including costs sanctions.

The categories are:

- *Small claim track* for cases involving up to £5,000 in England and Wales and cases involving over £5,000 with the parties consent, claims for personal injury where damages claimed do not exceed £1,000 and some claims by residential tenants. There are different financial limits in Scotland and Northern Ireland. A date is fixed for a preliminary or final hearing and directions for case management ensure the trial proceeds quickly and efficiently. Procedure is aimed at keeping costs to a minimum by dispensing with formalities and is designed for the litigant in person in the cases of debt claims, consumer disputes, accident claims, disputes about ownership of goods and some landlord and tenant disputes.

■ *Fast track* for cases involving over £5,000 and less than £15,000. There is a £275 trial fee, standard directions for trial preparation and a maximum of one day (five hours) for trial with, usually, no oral expert evidence and costs are fixed. Claims exceeding £15,000 are also allocated to fast track if the trial is likely to last for only one day and there is only one expert on each side in two areas of expertise.

■ *Multi track* for more complex cases and those involving over £15,000. There is a £500 trial fee, no standard procedure and a range of case management provisions, including standard directions, conferences and pre-trial reviews.

Local County Courts are listed in the telephone directory. You must usually sue in the court closest to where the defendant lives or carries on business, or where the incident on which the claim is based occurred. On a contract, you sue where the contract was concluded. If you choose the wrong court, the case is transferred at extra cost.

Time limits are basic. The court serves the proceedings on the defendant. If there is no response, you can ask for bailiff service or serve proceedings yourself. You must file the other documents in the proceedings with the court and serve them on the defendant yourself. You must therefore ask for acknowledgement of service (receipt) of documents that are 'served' the day following postage to the appropriate address by first-class post.

The claimant starts the action and the person sued is the defendant. It is not usually difficult to identify your opponent unless there are several possibilities, eg in a road accident claim you may want to sue the driver, car owner and/or the driver's employer. Multiple defendants pay in proportion to their liability.

Proceedings must be filed with the court and served on (ie delivered to) the defendant or his or her solicitor.

Service on a limited company is to the registered office or on senior management. Companies cannot litigate 'in person', but you can apply for an order permitting a director or officer to appear for the company. The Articles may require the consent of the board or the shareholders before proceedings brought by a company can be continued.

If partners or the partnership are sued, service is on the partner or person controlling or managing the partnership's principal place of business.

Someone using a trade name is served by naming them or the business premises and serving proceedings at the principal business premises. Individuals are served at their usual or last known address.

The names of directors and of up to 20 partners are on business documents and filed at Companies House. Partners must disclose their names and addresses to the court, whether sued personally or in the partnership name, and can be served personally or at the principal place of business.

The first step is to complete a claim form with the names and addresses of the parties, concise details of the claim and why you are taking action, and a statement of value together with a statement of truth as to its contents. If you need to set out the facts at length, they must be contained in a separate document – the particulars of claim. If sent separately, it must be filed with the Court Office within 14 days of serving the claim form on the defendant, together with its own statement of truth.

The County Court is not strict about form and in a straightforward claim for debt, 'I claim £X the price of goods sold and delivered to Y on...', is sufficient, but usually pleadings refer to claimant *and* defendant: 'the claimant claims £X'. Other claims require more details, eg road accident particulars must list the date, place and circumstances of the accident, say why the defendant was responsible and whether, as a result, you suffered pain, injury, loss or damage. If suing a driver's employer because the driver was working at the time of the accident, you must state that the driver was 'acting in the course of his/her employment'. Expenses and loss of earnings must also be listed; 'The claimant claims damages limited to £X' covers only general compensation assessed by the court. Interest may be awarded if included in the particulars.

A payment in or offer to settle made in writing 'and without prejudice except as to costs' by either party may dispose of the claim. An offer can be made at any time but payment in cannot be made before proceedings have issued. Thereafter, offer or payment in can be made any time before judgment, but, if not accepted, it must not be disclosed to the judge until after judgment but before costs are dealt with. If judgment exceeds the payment, the defendant pays the claimant's costs, but if he guessed right or judgment is for less, the defendant pays costs to the date of payment and the claimant pays both sides' costs thereafter.

You can apply for summary judgment even if the defendant has filed an acknowledgement of service or a defence. You must file written evidence with the court to support your claim, together with a statement of truth, file it with the court and serve it on the defendant. If no defence is served, you may have to wait until the hearing before you find out whether the defendant admits, defends and/or counterclaims, or whether there is a 'set-off' – eg for storage charges. If there is an arguable defence, the debtor may be permitted to defend on conditions – eg that all or part of the amount is paid into court pending trial. If there is a good defence, no conditions are imposed. If, however, the defendant admits the debt or you obtain judgment, the debt is entered on the Register of County Court Judgments and cancelled if paid within a month. Otherwise it stays on for six years and, when the court is notified of payment, it is noted against the entry.

The defendant may, however, make an offer to pay by instalments. If you reject instalment payments of a debt of less than £50,000, a court officer can decide without a hearing whether or not it should be accepted, taking into account the defendant's statement of means, other relevant information and your objections. If the officer does not make a decision, a judge will do so, with or without a hearing, and either party can apply to have the decision re-determined by a judge.

Judgment may be obtained without the defendant receiving notice of proceedings. The defendant must then immediately ask the court for details, producing the order for judgment. It is set aside if proceedings have not been properly served. Otherwise, it is set aside only if there is a reasonable defence and explanation for non-response and the defendant may have to pay costs to the date of judgment.

If you do not apply for summary judgment, the defence to a disputed claim must be filed with a statement of truth within 14 days. This can be extended to 28 days if the defendant instead files an acknowledgement of service within 14 days and files the defence 14 days thereafter.

Lists of relevant documents and other evidence are then exchanged and made available for inspection, including statements reports, photographs and sketch plans, unless otherwise ordered. 'Without prejudice' oral and written offers of settlement are excluded unless you choose to put them in evidence.

Agreement saves costs. For instance, you may be able to agree the cost of repairs instead of bringing witnesses to trial, leaving only liability for the trial.

The parties can ask for orders permitting them to act, or directing their opponent to do (or stop doing) something, pending the hearing. These applications are interlocutory and are made *inter partes* – on notice to the other side – at a fee of £35 – or, if urgent, *ex parte* – without notice –- at £65. Usually they must be served and filed, and the court office will tell you about time limits and restrictions. Some interlocutory orders, eg an injunction to stop someone trading, can be expensive because the court may require an undertaking to pay damages accruing until the hearing.

If costs are not agreed between the parties, the court will make 'detailed assessment' of costs at the end of the case. The court can, however, assess them on a summary basis at any stage and ask for estimates of accrued and future costs, and may order a payment on account of costs pending detailed assessment.

Costs are payable within 14 days of judgment unless the court orders otherwise and assessment is on a standard or indemnity basis.

Standard costs are those proportionate to the claim and reasonably incurred in the circumstances. Proportionality is not a factor in awarding costs on an indemnity basis. Whether standard or indemnity, the court takes into account the parties' conduct, the amount of money or property involved, its importance to the parties, the complexity of the case and the time, skill and specialised knowledge of those involved.

You may be able to appeal against a decision you think is wrong. The court office will inform you of time limits and explain procedures, but before appealing you should take legal advice.

Collecting debts after County Court litigation

When judgment is obtained, you can enlist the court's help in enforcing it at a cost of up to £95. County Court enforcement is confined to issue of:

- warrants;
- third party debt orders;
- charging orders;
- attachment of earnings orders;
- orders directing the transfer, delivery or recovery of possession of money or property.

Other enforcement proceedings must be taken in the High Court. This is often more successful because the County Court Bailiff's powers are more restricted than the High Court Sheriff's.

Unless stated to the contrary, stay of execution (delaying enforcement) is automatic for 14 days after money judgment is entered. An order to wind up a company stops execution on judgments against it.

A money judgment debtor can be ordered to attend court for examination as to property and means.

Warrants of execution are enforceable against goods. If located in several areas, concurrent warrants can issue in several courts. Costs are usually allowed and you should tell the court if you reach agreement with the debtor or withdraw from possession so the warrant can be suspended. If reissued, your priority is from the date of reissue.

Warrants are to enforce judgments or orders for recovery, or delivery of possession of land, and can issue 14 days after judgment or the day after a defendant is ordered to vacate. The court can suspend orders of possession for arrears of rent or under a mortgage and the warrant is cancelled on payment of arrears plus costs.

Delivery of goods is enforced by warrant of delivery or attachment. On assessed value, you can execute for the value, or judgment may permit retaining goods pending payment. Injunctions and orders are enforced by warrant of attachment.

A judgment debtor may be committed to prison if he or she has persistently and wilfully disobeyed an order. On a money judgment, you must show the debtor had means to pay since judgment.

Charging orders on a debtor's land are made to enforce money judgments. The charge is registrable at the Land Registry or under the Land Charges Act, but not under the Companies Act. Charging orders on company shares and debentures are made on judgments for fixed amounts and can include dividends and interest. You can also obtain a 'stop notice' or injunction, which effectively invalidates dealings.

Attachment of earnings orders are available against anyone in employment, whatever the amount of the debt. You must identify the employer. The debtor must give details of the employment and current and future earnings, resources and needs, and the employer may have to file a statement of the debtor's earnings. The order directs the employer to make deductions from pay and pay them to the court, which must be notified if the employment ends.

Any unconditional debt, even if not immediately payable, can be garnished if it accrues solely to the debtor. Current bank accounts can be attached and (on conditions) deposit accounts, but you may lose priority to a third party if attachment is not completed by payment before a petition for bankruptcy or winding up is lodged.

A third party debt order stops defendants taking money out of their bank or building society account. The money is paid from their account. The order can also be sent to anyone who owes the defendant money.

If you cannot use any other method, the court may agree to appoint a receiver. The order covers the sale proceeds of land or a share of rents and property held jointly or subject to a *lien* or trust. It can include an injunction ancillary or incidental to appointment if the debtor might dispose of the property. The receiver may have to give undertakings to the court or you may be made personally liable for his or her actions. The order does not make you a secured creditor, so it should be registered as a charge or caution if made against land.

Judgment is enforceable against the partnership's and the partners' property and against partners who were served in the proceedings or admitted in the proceedings that they were partners. Charging orders against a partner charge his or her interest in the partnership property, plus the partner's share of profits. By the same or a later order, a receiver can be appointed over other money due to the partner from the partnership and the court can make other orders and directions. The partner or his or her partners can redeem or purchase the charge if a sale is ordered.

The leave of the court is necessary before the partnership or a partner can enforce judgment against another partner.

Enforcement against a company is against the directors or other officers, but leave of the court is required before issue.

Non-compliance with a judgment or order is a ground for bankruptcy or winding up. But service of a statutory demand – which must be for at least £750 – often leads to payment of the amount due without recourse to litigation.

Statutory references

Arbitration Acts 1950, 1975, 1979 & 1996
Attachment of Earnings Act 1971
Civil Procedure Act 1997
Companies Acts 1985 & 1989
Consumer Credit Act 1974
County Courts Act 1984
Courts and Legal Services Act 1990
Criminal Justice Act 1982
Fair Trading Act 1973
Hire Purchase Act 1965
Insolvency Act 1986
Late Payment of Debts (Interest) Act 1998
Law Reform (Miscellaneous Provisions) Act 1934
Partnership Act 1890
Powers of the Criminal Court Act 1973
Supreme Court Act 1981

13

Bankruptcy and liquidation

Profit patterns fluctuate and projections are not always accurate. Before embarking on the sea of private enterprise, you should have some idea as to what happens if you run aground.

Insolvency

Insolvency is defined as:

- when debts and liabilities – including contingent and prospective – exceed assets;
- failure to pay a judgment debt (resulting from successful legal proceedings);
- failure to pay, compound or secure an undisputed debt of at least £750, within three weeks of formal demand, or if there is a serious possibility assets will be dissipated, forthwith;
- approval of a voluntary arrangement;
- the making of an administrative order;
- the appointment of an administrative receiver.

Only professionally qualified, licensed insolvency practitioners may act in bankruptcies and liquidations.

Contracts imposing unfair or oppressive rates of interest may be set aside by the court and onerous (oppressive) contracts for leaseholds can be disclaimed. If not registered under the Bills of Sale or Companies Act, general assignments of book debts are void, unless paid before presentation of a petition, the debts are due under specified contracts or were part of a transfer made in good faith and for value, or the transfer benefited the creditors.

Employees not given the proper period of notice of dismissal may be entitled to compensation from the Department of Trade and Industry consisting of the following, at a maximum of £290 per week:

- ■ up to 12 weeks' pay;
- ■ up to 8 weeks' arrears of pay; and
- ■ up to 6 weeks' holiday pay.

Voidable transactions, preferences and transactions at an undervalue

Sole traders and partnerships

Transactions putting creditors, sureties or guarantors into a better position than other creditors can be set aside as 'preferences', including transactions:

- ■ at an undervalue (ie gifts or transfers made for significantly less than market value or in consideration of marriage) – at risk if made less than five years before presentation of a petition for bankruptcy or an administrative order, *and* if intended to put assets beyond the reach or prejudice the interests of actual or potential creditors;
- ■ at a proper price – at risk for six months but two years if made with an 'associate'.

LLPs and companies

Voidable periods vary, dating back from presentation of a petition for an administration order, the date the order is made, or the commencement of winding up or liquidation, but:

- Transactions at an undervalue are safe if made in good faith, for business purposes and for the LLP's or company's benefit, but are voidable in a company liquidation if with a 'connected person' (see page 34).
- Preferences made when the LLP or company was insolvent or that cause insolvency are at risk for six months to two years.
- Floating charges are at risk for one or two years.

Trading with an intent to defraud creditors – which may include paying cheques into the LLP's or company's account after it stops trading – imposes unlimited liability on the designated partners or directors. In insolvent winding up or liquidation, designated partners or directors, *de facto* and shadow directors may be criminally liable and subject to disqualification for wrongful trading. The only defence is that every step was taken to minimise loss.

The voluntary procedures

Insolvent individuals and undischarged bankrupts who have not applied for 12 months, their trustee or the official receiver (a member of staff of the Department of Trade and Industry), can make arrangements with creditors through the court. Partnerships, LLPs and companies can also agree arrangements and compromises with creditors and apply for administration orders so business can be reorganised and insolvency avoided. There is now an additional voluntary arrangement for LLPs and small companies, allowing them to seek a moratorium (a temporary bar on creditors' claims) to give management time to put together a rescue scheme for the creditors' consideration. Until formal approval or rejection no legal action can be taken against business assets, but agreements in satisfaction of debts or approved schemes of arrangement are legally binding. Details of the procedure are on www.insolvency.gov.uk.

With partnerships, these voluntary arrangements can be used even if an insolvency order is made against the partnership or a partner but there must be interlocking arrangements if the partnership and the partners both want to agree arrangements.

Partners, the LLP, directors, liquidators or administrators put proposals and a statement of (financial) affairs to creditors – and in a company, shareholders – nominating a supervisor. There may be creditors' meetings, secured and preferred creditors are protected as in bankruptcy and liquidation, and on application the court can stay (stop) the proceedings. Disadvantages are that:

- creditors cannot recover VAT bad debt relief;
- until the order is made partners and directors remain at risk.

Administration orders are mainly used if there are no standard fixed and floating charges and the court must be satisfied that:

- the business is, or is likely to become, unable to pay its debts; or
- all or part of the business would survive as a going concern; or
- creditors are likely to agree a satisfactory arrangement; or
- realising the assets is likely to be more advantageous than a winding up.

The administration order can be used in conjunction with other voluntary arrangements but not in a liquidation.

The partnership and/or the partners, and/or the directors and/or the company, and/or creditors, or if the business is already being wound up the liquidator, can petition. Secured creditors and debenture holders must be notified and the petition can only be withdrawn with leave of the court.

The administrator takes over management but cannot prevent an application for dissolution or appointment of an administrative receiver (under a company's floating charge). Partners' and directors' powers are restricted, creditors' and shareholders' meetings may be called and a more detailed statement of affairs must be prepared, confirmed on affidavit by current and former partners or directors and in some cases those involved in the company's formation, and employees. The Registrar must be notified and details of the appointment must appear on business documents and in the

Gazette and in a newspaper that will bring it to the notice of creditors. Creditors and shareholders can apply to court if the business is, was, or will be, managed so they are unfairly prejudiced and the court can regulate the administration.

Administration ends on application to the court either because the purposes specified in the order cannot be carried out or because they have been completed.

Sole trader

Sole traders are personally liable for business debts and obligations. Personal assets, stock in trade and business assets can be sold. All you can keep are tools, books, vehicles and other equipment necessary for personal use in your business or employment and clothing, bedding, furniture and necessary provision for you and your family. But the trustee in bankruptcy can claim items he or she thinks will sell at more than replacement cost and you may have to pay over part of your earnings until discharge. The trustee, in whom some rights of (legal) action are vested, must be informed of increases in pay and estate (assets) but you can keep property held on trust for others and property payable under third party insurances.

Petitions in bankruptcy, bankruptcy orders and arrangements with creditors are registrable against real property and may bind a purchaser with unregistered title. They can be registered against registered property which stops dealings except through the official receiver or trustee.

Bankruptcy

The petition is presented by the debtor, creditor, supervisor, person acting in, or bound by, a voluntary arrangement, the official receiver, the Director of Public Prosecutions or person named in a Criminal Bankruptcy Order. Issue protects the debtor and his or her estate from legal proceedings and some legal processes. On a debtor's petition, the court may consider summary administration (for 'small' bankruptcies) and whether there should be a report.

An interim receiver or special manager takes over the debtor's estate pending appointment of a trustee, protecting assets and disposing of those liable to diminish in value. He or she continues to act in summary administration and criminal bankruptcy.

The debtor is then an undischarged bankrupt, deprived of ownership of most of his or her assets. He or she must cooperate with the receiver and hand over books and records. Except on the debtor's petition, a statement of affairs must be provided and there may be public examination in court and creditors' meetings.

Assets available include property acquired before and after the order, assets in voidable transactions and part of current income but the right of occupation of a solvent spouse and dependants is protected. Debts and interest must be proved. Secured creditors can realise or value the security and prove for the balance or surrender it and prove for the full amount. The trustee may continue the business and make periodic payments (dividends).

It is an offence for a bankrupt:

- not to have kept proper accounts for two years prior to the order;
- to have materially contributed to his or her financial problems by gambling;
- to take assets outside the jurisdiction;
- to make a false statement of affairs;
- to enter into a transaction intending to defraud creditors;
- to go into business in a name other than that stated in the order;
- to act as a director or be involved in company management – anyone acting on the bankrupt's instructions in relation to a company also commits an offence.

And the bankruptcy must be disclosed when applying for credit and accepting payment in advance.

The order of distribution is:

- liquidation costs;
- preferential debts proportionately, ie 12 months' PAYE and NICs, contributions relating to subcontractors in the construction industry, six months' VAT, betting duty, pension scheme contributions,

12 weeks' wage arrears if no notice given, otherwise 6 weeks, to a maximum of £205, and payments under the employment legislation;

■ secured creditors;
■ unsecured creditors plus interest until distribution;
■ provable debts plus interest due to the bankrupt's spouse.

Bankruptcy dates from the order and lasts until discharge but may be annulled if debts are paid off or secured. Discharge is automatic after three years for the first-time bankrupt, two years in summary administration. Otherwise it can be deferred for up to 15 years. The bankrupt can then go into business and, with some exceptions, is no longer liable for provable debts.

It is proposed that the period of disqualification be extended to 15 years if there was fraud or recklessness, and that if fraudsters seek a loan of more than £250 they will be required to tell the lender they are bankrupt, as well as their business contacts if they go into business under a new name.

Partnerships

Partners have complete financial commitment but commitment to co-partners ends by mutual agreement, dissolution, death and bankruptcy.

Dissolution by agreement is seldom straightforward and the agreement should set out terms applying to dissolution.

The partnership ends if business becomes illegal and unless the agreement states otherwise:

■ on completion of the undertaking or end of the period for which it was formed;
■ on a partner's bankruptcy, death, or resignation;
■ if a partner's share is charged by the court for personal debt – but the other partners can buy it and continue in business.

You can rescind (cancel) the agreement if there is fraud by a potential partner. You are entitled to damages for deceit, a lien (right of retention for the price) on surplus assets equal to your capital contribution, plus interest and costs, an indemnity against partnership debts and repayment of anything paid towards liabilities, plus interest.

Payment for a retiring or deceased partner's share substitutes the agreement to pay for the final account and distribution of assets but you should agree a formal settlement. (An option to purchase limits liability by the terms of the option.) Executors of deceased partners should ask the court to appoint a manager or receiver.

If losses are due to a partner, you can apply to the court – or, with an arbitration clause, the arbitrator – for dissolution on the ground that it is 'just and equitable'.

The court appoints a receiver or receiver and manager who is usually required to take the 'usual accounts and enquiries' and complete the dissolution. Receivers take in income and pay outgoings. Managers continue the business so receivers are usually appointed if the business is to be wound up.

Partners' responsibilities continue until winding up is concluded but only solvent or surviving partners are committed. When surviving partners of a deceased partner mortgage land, the deceased partner's estate may lose priority and the personal representatives should join in conveyances of land bought before 1926. If a partner is bankrupt, his trustee should be a party.

On dissolution, one partner sues in the partnership's name and distributes the assets. Goodwill must be sold unless otherwise agreed or it is personal and stays with the partners. If sold, they cannot solicit new business with existing connections. Except with a fixed-term partnership terminated by death, repayment of premiums can be ordered and when the assets are sold and the partnership dissolved a general account is made up in accordance with the partnership's usual practice.

Payments go first to preferential then secured creditors and then to pay other debts and liabilities. If there are insufficient partnership assets to pay off creditors, the shortfall ranks with the ordinary debts of the individual partners. Partners' advances come next, then winding up costs and initial capital contributions. If costs are not covered, they are paid proportionately by the partners. Losses, unless otherwise agreed, including capital losses, come from profits, then capital and then from the partners in accordance with their entitlement to share profits.

Insolvency

The law applying to sole traders applies with modifications to partners and partnerships but *not* to LLPs.

A petition served on a partner is served on the partnership which can be wound up without involving their insolvency but the adjudication order is made against the partners, not the partnership.

The partners (but not a limited partner), creditors or person acting in a voluntary arrangement can petition and the business is wound up as an unregistered company.

Partners, former partners and anyone who has or has had control or management is a director or officer under the insolvency and company directors' disqualification legislation with the liability of directors and management of a limited company.

If one or more partners as well as the partnership is insolvent there are two claims: first, between the partnership's and the partners' creditors if all partners are bankrupt; second, between a bankrupt partner's creditors and solvent co-partners.

If all the partners are bankrupt, creditors can claim against partnership assets and any unpaid balance comes from the partners' estates. Preferred creditors then rank with unsecured creditors but regain priority if payment is made into the joint estate from a partner's estate. Secured creditors can claim against the partnership or a partner without valuing the security. There are the following variations:

- If there are no partnership assets creditors can claim equally from each partner.
- Partners and the partnership are liable for their own fraudulent acts.
- Debts owed by the partnership and the partners can be claimed against the partnership and the partners.
- Creditors who put a partner into bankruptcy can usually also claim as partnership creditors.
- The trustees in bankruptcy of partners in business on their own account can claim against the partnership.
- Partnership creditors have priority over creditors of an insolvent corporate partner; the claims rank *pari passu* (proportionately) between themselves.

LLPs and companies

Receivership is when assets secured by a floating charge are realised and paid to the holder. Secured creditors can enforce the security without a winding up and without regard to anyone else's interests.

A company's outside investors' tax reliefs under the Enterprise Investment Scheme (EIS), Venture Capital Trust (VCT) or Corporate Venturing (CVS) scheme are not put at risk if, except for the actions of the receiver, the company still qualifies under the schemes.

Administrative receivers are appointed by debenture-holders or the court in accordance with the debenture. Their powers are similar to those administrators. Floating charges usually include a charge over plant and machinery which may also be covered by a fixed charge. If the company is in default before a winding up resolution, the charge becomes fixed, giving the lender priority over all the creditors. Notice of the appointment must be given to the company and creditors, and appear on company documents, in the *Gazette* and in a newspaper which will bring it to the creditors' notice. The administrative receiver prepares the fuller statement of affairs required in administration and reports to the Registrar and – unless he or she reports within three months – to secured creditors and their trustees and, if appointed, the liquidator. The appointment ends by court order or resignation.

Receivers are appointed under a fixed charge or by the court. They report to directors, shadow directors and the Registrar. If an administrator is appointed the security cannot be enforced without consent of the court or administrator but the fixed chargeholders retain priority if the security is sold. The appointment ends when the receiver has sufficient to pay his or her expenses and discharge the debt.

Voluntary liquidation

A member's (partner's or shareholders') voluntary liquidation is where a majority of the designated partners or directors produce a satisfactory declaration of solvency, setting out assets and liabilities and stating debts will be paid within 12 months. The partners or shareholders appoint a liquidator and the declaration is filed with the Registrar. If debts are not paid, the directors may be liable to a fine or imprisonment. Pending appointment of a liquidator, the directors cannot, without the consent of the court, do anything except what is necessary to protect company assets. Although the liquidator is not appointed or supervised by creditors most of his or her powers can only be exercised with the consent of the court until the creditors' meeting.

If there is no declaration, the liquidator disagrees with it or the debts are not paid, it becomes a creditors' voluntary liquidation. Creditors and shareholders nominate liquidators but the creditors' choice takes precedence. A creditors' committee which includes shareholders' representatives may also be appointed to supervise the liquidator. Directors, shareholders and creditors can nominate a joint or alternate liquidator through the court.

The liquidator realises the assets and distributes the proceeds but may need the consent of the court or the creditors' committee.

Outside investors' tax reliefs under the EIS or VCT Schemes are not put at risk in a liquidation.

Liquidation starts with the date of the winding up resolution and lasts until the liquidator vacates office after his or her final report to shareholders and creditors, but he or she can resign on notice to the Registrar of the final meeting.

All debts, present, future, certain and contingent, including quantified claims for damages, are provable unless the company is insolvent. Shareholders are only liable for the unpaid balance on their shares. The first payment is under fixed charges, then liquidation expenses, preferential debts, floating charges and arrears of dividends, with remaining assets going equally to unsecured creditors.

The company is dissolved three months from registration by the Registrar of the liquidator's final account and return.

Compulsory winding up

The LLP or a partner or partners can petition for compulsory winding up. In a company the company or contributories (ie shareholders who have held shares since incorporation or for 6 of the 18 months before liquidation) can lodge the petition. In both LLPs and companies the petition can also be lodged by creditors, the Secretary of State for Trade and Industry, the Financial Services Authority or the official receiver.

The court orders compulsory liquidation if:

■ the LLP or company has not started trading within a year of incorporation or has stopped trading for 12 months;
■ the LLP or company is insolvent;
■ the Secretary of State for Trade and Industry requests it.

And in a company if:

■ a special resolution requests it;
■ it is 'just and equitable' to do so;
■ a director or seller of shares to the company for capital requests it on the ground that it cannot pay its debts;
■ there is mismanagement or deadlock on the board but this applies only if the court is satisfied that voluntary liquidation is not in the interest of creditors or shareholders.

On making the order the directors' powers cease and the official receiver or provisional liquidator is appointed pending appointment of the liquidator. Details must appear on company documents, be notified to the Registrar and be advertised in the *Gazette* and two local newspapers.

Liquidation starts from presentation of the petition unless there was a voluntary liquidation, when it dates from the date of the resolution. A full statement of affairs may be required and no proceedings can be taken by or against the company without the consent of the court. There may be creditors' and shareholders' meetings. Appointment of the liquidator is as in a creditors' winding up but the official receiver can apply for appointment and creditors and contributories may appoint a liquidation committee. The liquidator realises and distributes the assets and must keep the official receiver informed. The official receiver may report to the court and apply for public examination of anyone involved in the company's affairs. The court can also order examination of company officers.

Penalties

Sole traders and partners can now be convicted for fraudulent trading. Anyone involved in trading with an intent to defraud, incurring debts without a reasonable prospect of repayment, or convicted for an indictable offence (serious and triable by jury) relating to the LLP or company or their assets may be prosecuted and disqualified from participating directly or indirectly in the management of an LLP or company for up to 15 years. Gross incompetence and 'commercial immorality' (including failure to carry out statutory duties) also brings disqualification. Offenders may also be fined up to £5,000 and/or face up to seven years' imprisonment.

If the company bought shares within a year of the winding up and cannot meet debts and liabilities, management may share liability for loss with the holder of the shares.

A member of an LLP who is disqualified cannot be a company director, nor can a disqualified director be a member of an LLP. Directors and shadow directors cannot, without court consent within 12 months of insolvent liquidation act for, or be involved in the promotion, formation or management of, or be connected with, a company with the same name, or use a former name or trading name used during the previous 12 months, or one which suggests continuing association for five years.

Distribution is as in a voluntary liquidation except charges over distrained goods are paid after floating charges.

The official receiver can apply for early dissolution if expenses will not be paid. Otherwise the liquidator reports to creditors and the company is dissolved three months after dissolution is registered.

Statutory references

Attachment of Earnings Act 1971
Bills of Sale Act 1878
Companies Acts 1985 and 1989
Company Directors Disqualification Act 1986
Consumer Credit Acts 1979 and 2006
Employment Protection (Consolidation) Act 1978
Fraud Act 2006

Insolvency Act 1986
Insolvency Act (No. 2)1994
Land Charges Act 1972
Land Registration Act 1925
Limited Liability Partnership Act 2000
Limited Partnership Act 1907
Matrimonial Homes Act 1983
Partnership Act 1890
Powers of Criminal Courts Act 1973

14

Takeovers and mergers

Business is good, profits are climbing, management is efficient – now is the time to consider expansion. But you may also be taking on:

- outstanding and transferred liability for VAT;
- employees' existing and continuing holiday entitlement;
- employees' accrued rights on unfair dismissal and redundancy *but* they lose their rights if they refuse to work for you.

If the first move on acquisition is to rationalise by dismissing employees, dismissal is automatically unfair if the reason or principal reason is the takeover. But you can fairly dismiss for 'an economic, technical or organisational reason entailing changes in the workforce'. Even on fair dismissal, there may be entitlement to redundancy payments. You should therefore obtain an indemnity from your seller to cover any claim which might arise on transfer of the business.

The sole trader and expansion

The route to expansion is by way of taking on investors, partners or incorporating yourself as a limited company.

Mergers

There is a new test for unlawful mergers: if there is, or may be, a 'substantial lessening of competition' the merger may be prohibited. The Office of Fair Trading and the Competition Commission make the decision. Ministers are also involved if there are public interest issues involved, such as national security.

Partnerships

When taking on additional partners or amalgamating with another firm, you must change the partnership name and the partnership agreement should be amended to reflect your extended liability for new partners. Existing and incoming partners should elect for continuance, thereby avoiding assessment to tax on the basis that the partnership stopped trading and started again when you took on new partners. Incoming partners should confirm the partnership's mandate with the bank and should be joined as co-sureties to the bank guarantee. You may also want to extend their liability to cover contracts with the partnership's existing creditors – by replacing the original contracts which include them – and if they should share in existing book debts.

LLPs

LLPs must in addition comply with the Limited Liability Partnership, Companies and Insolvency Acts, and before proceeding you should take legal and financial advice.

Companies

Company amalgamations must also comply with the Companies and Insolvency Acts and again you require legal and financial advice.

Share for share and part cash offers

You can make a bid for a company in return for shares which are distributed to the selling company's shareholders in accordance with their rights. You can also make an offer extended generally to all the shareholders with part payment in your shares and the balance in cash. The offer is usually conditional on the acceptance of at least three-quarters of the shareholders, holding not less than 90 per cent of the shares – because you are usually bound to acquire the remaining 10 per cent on the same terms, unless the court orders otherwise on a shareholder's application. Bids can be confined to one class of shares, if your company already holds nine-tenths of that class of shares. If acceptances exceed the offer, you must take shares, *pro rata,* from all accepting shareholders.

The procedure for mergers and reconstructions involving a new issue of shares at a premium are set out on page 33.

You can transfer assets from one company to another on a tax neutral basis. Transfer is on a no gain/no loss basis and can consist of a disposal of the whole or part of a business to another company as part of a scheme of reconstruction or amalgamation, but the assets must remain within the scope of UK taxation.

There is a 0.5 per cent Stamp Duty on sales of shares and other securities, but there are reliefs for certain company reorganisations where there is no significant change of underlying ownership.

Straightforward exchange of shares between buying and selling companies, when you are not seeking further capital, is usually done by issuing your shares to the selling company's shareholders. If a majority of the selling company's shareholders accept, the selling company's shares are cancelled, except for any your company is to hold, and the selling company's shareholders receive your shares in payment for theirs. Payment can be in cash instead of shares if the reserve created by cancellation of the shares is capitalised. This is then applied to pay up further shares in the selling company, which are issued to you in place of the cancelled shares. The result is the same as a share-for-share takeover by compulsory acquisition but the majority necessary to approve the takeover is smaller and the court, creditors and shareholders must approve the arrangement.

Taking over while raising capital

If you are seeking more capital, the selling company must be wound up and its shareholders must make further contributions of capital. A new company is formed and the selling company sells its undertaking through its liquidator in return for shares in the new company. Shareholders receive your shares or they can be given partly paid-up shares in return for the fully paid shares they previously held which means they take on a fresh liability for calls or give up their rights to the new shares.

Varying shareholders' and creditors' rights

Three-quarters of the shareholders or creditors – in number and value – must consent if their rights are to be varied. They can object within 21 days to the court, which can amend, vary, confirm or overrule the scheme. A selling company wanting to persuade its shareholders or creditors to agree to a sale must also apply to the court. The court monitors both these procedures and can order compensation for dissenting shareholders.

Directors' compensation for loss of office

Directors' compensation for loss of office must be approved by the selling company's shareholders or as specified in the Articles, otherwise the directors are liable to prosecution and the compensation belongs to shareholders, even if payment is made within a year before, or two years after, the takeover offer. The Company Directors' Performance and Compensation Bill currently before Parliament requires the board to take performance into account, whatever is in the service contract, and to disclose the payment on a shareholder's request and if it exceeds the previous 12 months' basic salary, to include it in the annual report with an explanation of the amount.

The first £30,000 is not taxable and a reduced rate of tax applies up to £50,000. Tax is payable at the full rate on the balance. Payments for shares to directors exceeding the price paid to other shareholders are also considered to be compensation, unless the bid is only for *de facto* control by acquisition of less than a third of voting shares, when the directors are not accountable to shareholders, although they may be liable to the company. They can, however, keep genuine payments for premature determination of service contracts or as a pension for past services.

Statutory references

Companies Act 1985 and 1989
Employment Protection (Consolidation) Act 1978
Income and Corporation Taxes Act 1970 (as amended)
Insolvency Act 1986
Limited Liability Partnership Act 2002
Partnership Act 1890
Registration of Business Names Act 1916
Transfer of Undertakings Regulations 2006

Appendix: Useful addresses

Advisory, Conciliation and Arbitration Service (ACAS)
286 Euston Road
London NW1 3JJ
Tel: 08457 47 47 47
Website: www.acas.org.uk

The Bar Council
289–293 High Holborn
London WC1V 7HZ
Tel: 020 7242 0082

British Franchise Association
Thames View
Newton Road
Henley-on-Thames
Oxfordshire RG9 1HG
Tel: 01491 578 050
Website: www.british-franchise.org.
uk

British Insurance Brokers Association (BIBA)
BIBA House
14 Bevis Marks
London EC3A 7NT
Tel: 0870 950 1790
Fax: 020 7626 9676
Website: www.biba.org.uk

Business Link
A DTI service providing practical
help and advice at local offices
Available online at www.
businesslink.gov.uk

Centre for Effective Dispute Resolution
Exchange Tower
1 Harbour Exchange
London E14 9GB
Tel: 020 7536 6000
Fax: 020 7536 6001
Website: www.cedr.co.uk

Chartered Institute of Arbitrators
International Arbitration and
Mediation Centre
12 Bloomsbury Square
London WC1A 2LP
Tel: 020 7421 7444

Companies House addresses
English/Welsh companies
Companies House
Crown Way
Cardiff CF14 3UZ
Tel: 029 2038 0801
Website: www.companieshouse.org.
uk

There are also offices in Birmingham,
Leeds and Manchester

Scottish companies
Companies House
37 Castle Terrace
Edinburgh EH1 2EB
Tel: 0870 333 3636

Central enquiries for all branches
Tel: 0870 333 3636
Fax: 029 2038 0801

Department of Trade and Industry
1 Victoria Street
London SW1H 0ET
Tel: 020 7215 6740
Website: www.dti.gov.uk

**Export Credits Guarantee
Department**
2 Exchange Tower
PO Box 2200
Harbour Exchange Square
London E14 9GS
Tel: 020 7512 7000
Fax: 020 7512 7649
Website: www.ecgd.gov.uk

Health and Safety Executive
HSE infoline
Rose Court
2 Southwark Bridge
London SE1 9HS
Tel: 0845 345 0055
Website: www.hse.gov.uk

HM Courts Service
Customer Service Unit
5th Floor, Clive House
Petty France
London SW1H 9HD
Tel: 020 7189 2000/0845 456 8770

HPI Ltd (Hire purchase information
– motor vehicles)
Dolphin House
New Street
Salisbury
Wiltshire SP1 2PH
Tel: 01722 422422
Website: www.hpi.co.uk

Information Commissioner (data protection)
England and Wales
Information Commissioner's Office
Wycliffe House
Water Lane
Wilmslow
Cheshire SK9 5AF
Tel: 01625 545 740
Fax: 01625 524 510
Website: www.information-commissioner.gov.uk

Scotland
Scottish Information Commissioner
Kinburn Castle
Doubledyke Road
St Andrews
Fife KY16 9DS
Tel: 01334 464610
Fax: 01334 464611
Website: www.itspublilcknowledge.info

Institute of Directors
116 Pall Mall
London SW1Y 5ED
Tel: 020 7839 1233

Insurance Ombudsman (now part of the Financial Ombudsman Service)
South Quay Plaza
183 Marsh Wall
London E14 9SR
Tel: 020 7964 1000
Fax: 020 7964 1001
Website: www.financial-ombudsman.org.uk

Land Registry
Tel: 020 7917 8888
Website: www.landreg.gov.uk
Land registry searches online: www.landsearch.me.uk

The Law Society
113 Chancery Lane
London WC2A 1PL
Tel: 020 7242 1222

Register of Judgments, Orders and Fines
171–172 Cleveland Street
London W1T 6QR
Tel: 020 7380 0133
Website: www.registry-trust.org.uk

Royal Institution of Chartered Surveyers
RICS Contact Centre
Surveyor Court
Westwood Way
Coventry CV4 8JE
Tel: 0870 333 1600

The Stationery Office (TSO)
PO Box 29
Norwich NR3 1GN
Tel: 0870 600 5522
Website: www.tso.co.uk

UK Patent Office

Main Office

The Patent Office

Concept House

Cardiff Road

Newport

South Wales NP10

London Office

Harmsworth House

13–15 Bouverie Street

London EC4Y 8DP

Tel: 08459 500 505

Fax: 01633 813 600

Index

Index of advertisers

Also available in *The Sunday Times Business Enterprise* series, published by Kogan Page

The Business Plan Workbook, 5th edition, by Colin Barrow, 2005
Financial Management for the Small Business by Colin Barrow, 2006
Forming a Limited Company, 9th edition, by Patricia Clayton, 2006
How to Prepare a Business Plan, 4th edition (revised), by Edward Blackwell, 2004
Raising Finance by Paul Barrow, 2004
Starting a Successful Business, 5th edition, by Michael J Morris, 2005
The Strategic Planning Workbook, 2nd edition, by Neville Lake, 2006

The above titles are available from all good bookshops. For further information on these and other Kogan Page titles, or to order online, visit Kogan Page on the web at **www.kogan-page.co.uk**